PUPUS...
PLUS!

To my friends, named and unnamed,

who have shared their favorite recipes

with me over the years. Thank you

from the bottom of our hearts.

Lynn and I love you all.

PUPUS...
PLUS!

SACHI FUKUDA

3565 Harding Ave. Honolulu, HI 96816   808.734.7159   www.besspress.com

Design, food styling and photography by Karen Jones

Author photo courtesy of Hawaiian Electric Company, Inc.

Library of Congress Cataloging-in-Publication Data

Fukuda, Sachi.
    Pupus . . . plus / Sachi Fukuda.
    p. cm.
    Includes illustrations.
    ISBN 1-57306-229-4
    1. Cookery, Hawaiian.
    2. Appetizers - Hawaii. I. Title.
    TX724.5.H3.F85 2004 941.5-dc21

Printed in China

PUPUS...
PLUS!

PUPUS, SAUCES and DRESSINGS

MARINATED SHRIMP with ORANGES page 18

■ CURRIED FRUIT RELISH

This is an interesting alternative to meat and seafood pupus. This relish has a refreshing flavor and looks very nice when served.

1 can (1 pound 13 ounces)
   sliced peaches
1 can (1 pound 13 ounces)
   apricot halves
1 can (1 pound) pear halves
1 can (1 pound 4 ounces)
   pineapple chunks
$3/_4$ cup firmly packed
   brown sugar
2 to 3 teaspoons
   curry powder
$1/_3$ cup melted butter

Drain fruit thoroughly on paper towels. Place fruit in $2^{1}/_{2}$-quart casserole. Mix rest of ingredients and pour over fruit. Bake uncovered for 45 minutes at 350 degrees, turning gently once or twice.

■ If you like a little crunch in your fruits, use dried fruits in one-half the quantity with double the seasoning.

■ MONICA'S SALSA

2 tablespoons minced garlic
$1/_2$ bunch cilantro leaves
1 16-ounce jar mild salsa
4 tablespoons distilled
   vinegar
3 tablespoons sugar
4 medium tomatoes,
   coarsely chopped
Salt and pepper to taste

In food processor blend minced garlic and chopped cilantro leaves. Add salsa and vinegar, sugar, and 3 coarsely chopped tomatoes; blend. Add last coarsely chopped tomato until just blended, leaving chunks visible. Salt and pepper to taste. Refrigerate until time to serve.

■ SAMOSA

This is a family favorite of the Matsuuras', who lived in India for many years. Dr. Ruth made this for gatherings of family and friends. This recipe makes about 100 samosas, which can be frozen and fried at some later date. When preparing the samosas, lay them flat on a cookie sheet and cover each layer with waxed paper to prevent sticking. The won ton pi tends to melt after it is filled. When freezing the samosas, place them on a cookie sheet without overlapping and place in freezer. Once samosas are frozen, store in zip lock bags. To keep pieces from sticking together, don't overlap the samosas when thawing.

2 pounds unpeeled
   potatoes
2 pounds frozen peas
2 cups cilantro leaves,
   chopped
1/3 cup lemon juice
1 1/2 tablespoons
   curry powder
1 tablespoon salt
2 teaspoons ground
   black pepper
1 tablespoon ground cumin
1 tablespoon ground
   coriander
100 won ton pi wrappers
Vegetable oil for frying

Boil potatoes until done. Drain, place in bowl with frozen peas, and cover. When potatoes are cool enough to handle, remove potatoes, dice, return to bowl, and and mix with peas. Add chopped cilantro. In separate bowl, mix lemon juice with curry powder, salt, black pepper, cumin, and coriander. Add this mixture to potatoes and peas and mix well.

Spoon a heaping tablespoonful on each won ton pi, seal edges with water, and deep-fry in hot oil until nicely browned.

Serve with salsa or with shoyu and mustard mix.

■ JUANITA'S MARINATED MUSHROOMS

½ cup salad oil
⅓ cup cider vinegar
2 tablespoons chopped
    green onion
2 tablespoons chopped
    parsley
1 clove garlic, minced
½ teaspoon salt
2 teaspoons sugar
20 small mushrooms, sliced
1 small round onion,
    thinly sliced
2 cucumbers, thinly sliced

Combine all ingredients and marinate in refrigerator 8 hours.

■ SMOKED SALMON SPREAD

5 ounces smoked salmon, shredded

1³/₄ teaspoons horseradish

6 ounces cream cheese

1 tablespoon + 2 teaspoons lemon juice

¹/₂ teaspoon seasoned salt

¹/₂ teaspoon garlic salt

Cream together above ingredients until well blended. Serve with raw vegetables or crackers.

■ WARABI-SALMON PŪPŪ

1 tray salted salmon
   (³/₄ to I pound)
1 bunch young warabi (fern
   tips; tips should be tight)
3 tablespoons salt
3 large, firm ripe tomatoes,
   cubed
1 medium Maui onion,
   thinly sliced and chopped
   into ¹/₂-inch pieces

Rinse salted salmon 3 times and soak in ice water for 4 to 5 hours to dilute salt. Skin, bone, and cut salmon into ¹/₂-inch strips and ¹/₂-inch cubes. Squeeze out any liquid remaining in salmon. (Reserve this liquid to add if recipe needs more salt at the very end.) Refrigerate while preparing remaining ingredients.

Wash warabi and clean off fine hair that runs the length of the warabi by sticking your thumbnail into the groove. Cut into 1-inch pieces and blanch in pot of boiling water with 3 tablespoons salt for 45 seconds, stirring constantly. Drain and immediately soak in a bowl of water with ice cubes. After ice has melted, drain.

Mix salmon and tomatoes and onion. Add well-drained warabi and mix well. Refrigerate until ready to serve.

■ Warabi must be mixed immediately after draining. If left in the refrigerator for any length of time without mixing, it will turn dark. If it needs to be kept for any length of time after cooking, place it in a bowl filled with water. Drain and mix when ready to use.

■ BEST CRAB CAKES

1 teaspoon olive oil
½ cup chopped red pepper
½ cup chopped green pepper
½ cup chopped yellow
   pepper
1 teaspoon Tabasco
2 cups deboned and
   chopped king crab meat
2 tablespoons mayonnaise
4 egg whites
½ chopped jalapeno
   pepper
¼ cup chopped cilantro
½ cup panko (Japanese
   bread crumbs) +
   additional for dipping

Sauce
¼ cup horseradish
½ cup orange marmalade

Heat oil and sauté peppers. Add Tabasco to fried peppers and mix into crabmeat. Add mayonnaise, egg whites, jalapeno pepper, and cilantro. Add panko and if desired additional Tabasco. Shape into patties, dip in flour, and then in more panko. Fry in hot oil. Serve with sauce on the side.

■ CRAB REISLING

4 tablespoons butter
4 cups chicken broth
2 cups Reisling
¼ cup green onion
   or chives, thinly sliced
6 slices fresh ginger
1 tablespoon soy sauce
1 tablespoon lemon juice
3 pounds crab legs
   and claws

Heat butter over medium heat; add broth, wine, chives or green onion, ginger, soy sauce, and lemon juice. Bring to a boil, reduce heat, cover, and simmer 10 minutes. Add crab. Cover and simmer until heated through, about 10 to 15 minutes. Discard ginger and serve.

■ FRESH SHIITAKE MUSHROOMS
with PORK HASH

24 large, fresh
    shiitake mushrooms
1/2 pound lean ground
    pork or turkey
8 water chestnuts, minced
1 clove garlic, minced
1 tablespoon soy sauce
1 tablespoon sherry
1/2 teaspoon sugar
1 teaspoon cornstarch
1/4 teaspoon salt
Vegetable oil for frying
1/2 cup chicken broth
1 tablespoon oyster sauce

Clean mushrooms and remove stems. Mince stems and combine with ground pork or turkey, water chestnuts, and garlic. Add soy sauce, sherry, sugar, cornstarch, and salt. Mix well. Spoon 1 tablespoon filling into each mushroom cap.

Heat a little oil in a large skillet. Place mushrooms in pan, filled side up. Brown for 1 minute. Add stock, cover, and simmer for 15 minutes. Uncover and add oyster sauce to pan. Baste each mushroom with a little of sauce. Serve hot.

■ 'AHI POKE DIP

2 cups mayonnaise
½ cup chopped pickled
  ginger
½ cup chopped green onion
½ cup chopped cilantro
2 tablespoons lemon juice
½ cup soy sauce
2 teaspoons white pepper
½ teaspoon Worcestershire
  sauce
½ cup toasted sesame seeds
1 cup fresh 'ahi, chopped

Mix all ingredients except toasted sesame seeds and 'ahi. Chill everything until ready to serve. Mix in sesame seeds and 'ahi just before serving. Mixture can be refrigerated for up to a week. Lemon flavor gets stronger as it keeps, so use more or less according to your preference.

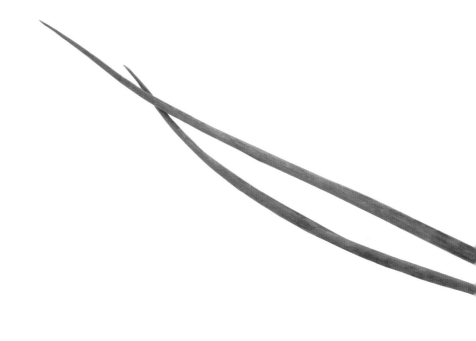

■ ROY'S WASABI NORI WRAPPED 'AHI with SAKE SOY PONZU SAUCE

When I told Roy Yamaguchi how much friends enjoyed the dish, he was kind enough to let me use his recipe. The dipping sauce alone is worth the effort. The recipe below is modified slightly from Roy's original; I used 8 ounces sashimi, but I used less of some of the other ingredients.

8 ounces sashimi, cut in a
   1-inch block
2 tablespoons wasabi paste
5 sheets nori
½ of 1.9-ounce jar furikake
4 tablespoons white sesame
   seeds
½ of 4-ounce package panko
   (Japanese bread crumbs)
1 cup mochiko rice flour
2 eggs, beaten
Vegetable oil for frying

Lightly coat 'ahi with wasabi. Heat nori sheet on stove. Wrap 'ahi with nori, using water to seal end. Mix furikake, sesame seeds, and panko. Set aside. Roll 'ahi in mochiko, dip in egg, and then roll in panko mixture, pressing panko into 'ahi roll.

Heat oil in frying pan on medium heat. Fry each side until panko turns golden brown, about 25 seconds on each side. Place on paper towel to drain. Cool slightly and cut into 1/2-inch slices. 'Ahi should be rare inside.

Sake Soy Ponzu Sauce

1 cup daikon, peeled, diced
2 tablespoons lemon juice
2 tablespoons lime juice
3 tablespoons hot
   sesame oil
½ cup mirin (sweet
   rice wine)
1½ cups low-sodium
   soy sauce

In a blender, puree daikon with lemon and lime juice until smooth. Add remaining ingredients and blend well.

■ This sauce is wonderful both as a salad dressing and as a dipping sauce.

■ FESTIVE OYSTERS

24 tiny oysters
4 tablespoons butter
1 large clove garlic,
    finely minced
2 tablespoons minced
    shallots
1½ tablespoons fresh
    lemon juice
Salt and pepper to taste
¾ cup fresh bread crumbs
4 tablespoons minced
    parsley
4 slices diced crisp bacon

Place half shells on a baking dish. In skillet melt butter; sauté garlic and shallots for 1 minute. Stir in lemon juice, salt, and pepper.

In small bowl mix bread crumbs and parsley; spread over oysters. Drizzle butter over (1 tablespoon per oyster) and add a little bit of crisp bacon. Cover and refrigerate until ready to serve. Bake at 375 degrees for 20 minutes. Broil until brown and serve.

■ MARINATED SHRIMP with ORANGES

5 pounds shelled shrimp, blanched
2 large onions, thinly sliced
1 cup cider vinegar
¼ cup ketchup
½ cup lemon juice
¾ cup olive oil
1 clove garlic, crushed
¼ cup sugar
½ teaspoon pepper
1 tablespoon salt
2 tablespoons mustard seed
2 tablespoons ground pepper flakes
1 teaspoon celery salt
½ teaspoon cayenne pepper
2 tablespoons minced parsley
1 11-ounce can mandarin oranges

Combine all ingredients except mandarin oranges and marinate in refrigerator for 3 days. Drain and add mandarin oranges just before serving.

■ This is a very colorful dish with a surprising flavor. You'll like it and serve it often.

■ THE VERY BEST SHRIMP COCKTAIL

This is the best cocktail sauce ever, with just enough zip to make you want more.

5 pounds shrimp
Juice from 1 lemon

Peel shrimp, devein, and cook in boiling water into which the juice of 1 lemon has been added. Once shrimp first turn white, they are done. Do not overcook. Drain, cool to room temperature, and refrigerate until ready to serve.

Cocktail Sauce
2 cups chili sauce
1½ cups tomato ketchup
½ cup prepared horseradish
3 tablespoons lemon juice
1 teaspoon salt
1 teaspoon Worcestershire
   sauce
Dash hot pepper sauce or
   Tabasco sauce

Mix all ingredients and chill until ready to serve.

■ BROILED STUFFED SHRIMP

2 pounds extra-large
   (16 to 20 per pound) shrimp
2 tablespoons minced
   green onion
¼ cup minced water
   chestnuts
¼ cup minced bamboo
   shoots
½ cup minced shiitake
   mushrooms
½ cup minced ham or
   turkey ham
1 teaspoon Worcestershire
   sauce
1 cup mayonnaise
¼ teaspoon seasoned salt
¼ teaspoon garlic salt
1 tablespoon + 1 teaspoon
   grated round onion

Clean shrimp, remove shells, and devein, leaving tails intact. Butterfly shrimp by cutting down center of shrimp's back from head to tail, almost all the way through. To prevent shrimp from curling during cooking, lightly score flesh on cut side, without cutting through. Tu rn over so that cut side is facing down. Refrigerate until ready to serve.

Combine remaining ingredients. Tu rn shrimp over and place a heaping tablespoonful of stuffing on each flattened, butterflied shrimp. This dish may be made a day ahead and refrigerated. Place waxed paper between layers when storing in refrigerator. Seal with plastic wrap to prevent shrimp from drying out. When ready to serve, broil in a single layer for 8 to 9 minutes or until stuffing is nicely browned.

■ ITALIAN BROILED SHRIMP

1 pound large (21 to 30 per
   pound) shrimp, shelled
2 tablespoons flour
4 tablespoons butter
¼ cup olive oil

Drawn Butter Sauce
4 tablespoons butter
2 tablespoons flour
Salt and freshly ground
   pepper to taste
1½ to 2 teaspoons fresh
   lemon juice
1 cup hot water
2 tablespoons finely
chopped garlic
¼ cup freshly chopped
   parsley
½ teaspoon oregano

Dust shrimp generously with flour. Melt butter in a flat broiling pan under broiler. Add oil and heat until bubbly. Place shrimp in pan and coat with butter-oil mixture. Broil for 3 minutes; shrimp will not be completely cooked.

To prepare drawn butter sauce, melt 2 tablespoons butter in a medium-sized saucepan over medium heat. Add flour, salt, and pepper and stir well. Whisk in lemon juice and water. Cook 5 minutes. Add remaining 2 tablespoons butter and stir until melted. Just before removing from heat, add garlic, parsley, and oregano. Heat another minute. Add broiled shrimp and stir until shrimp are evenly coated. Return shrimp to broiler. Broil under high heat 3 to 4 minutes or just until shrimp turns pink.

Serve with plenty of French bread to soak up this marvelous sauce.

■ SHRIMP WITH BACON

1 pound large (21 to 30 per
   pound) shrimp, shelled
4 slices bacon, cut into
   4 pieces each

Sauce
1/2 teaspoon salt
1/2 teaspoon cornstarch
1/2 teaspoon wine
1 tablespoon soy sauce

Batter
1 egg
1/4 teaspoon salt
6 tablespoons flour
2 tablespoons water or milk

Marinate shrimp in sauce for 15 minutes. Drain. Make small slit through back of each shrimp and slip in a piece of bacon. Dip into batter and deep-fry. Serve hot.

■ SHRIMP WITH NORI

1 pound large (21 to 30 per
  pound) shrimp
1/2 teaspoon ginger wine
  (wine soaked with grated
  ginger, drained, and
  measured)
1/2 teaspoon +
  1/3 teaspoon salt
1 container surimi■
  (fishcake base)
2 ounces water chestnuts,
  chopped
1 tablespoon chopped
  green onion
1 teaspoon sake
1/2 tablespoon sugar
1/4 teaspoon sesame oil
6 sheets nori

Clean, shell, and devein shrimp, leaving tails intact. Soak in ginger wine and 1/2 teaspoon salt for 20 minutes. Mix surimi and water chestnuts; add chopped green onion, sake, 1/3 teaspoon salt, sugar, and sesame oil. Cut each nori sheet into 4 pieces; place tablespoonful surimi in middle of nori piece. Place shrimp on top and cover with another tablespoonful surimi. Fold nori to wrap shrimp, leaving some tail exposed.

Heat oil and deep-fry shrimp over medium heat for 2 minutes. Tu rn shrimp over and cook another 2 minutes. Drain and serve.

■ If prepared surimi is unavailable, purchase 1 tray of Chinese fishcake mix and add 1/4 cup cornstarch and 1/4 cup water. Mix well and you are ready to go.

SAUCES and DRESSINGS

■ MISO YAKI SAUCE

½ cup miso
¼ cup sugar
1½ tablespoons shoyu
¾ tablespoon rice vinegar
¼ cup sake or sherry
2 green onions, minced
1-inch sliver ginger, minced

Mix all ingredients and pour over fish or chicken. Broil in oven or fry in a nonstick skillet lined with foil until nicely browned.

■ SWEET-SOUR BARBEQUE SAUCE

1 14-ounce bottle ketchup
1 8-ounce can tomato sauce
1 cup cider vinegar
½ teaspoon Worcestershire
  sauce
1 teaspoon Colman's
  mustard
1 teaspoon ground ginger
1 cup brown sugar
1 cup white sugar

Combine all ingredients and cook for 45 minutes. Stir occasionally to prevent burning. Wonderful with kālua pork sandwich or simmered in a pot or baked in the oven with any meat.

■ SOMEN SALAD SAUCE

This is a pleasant sauce – not too rich or too oily.

2 tablespoons sugar
1 teaspoon salt
¼ cup salad oil
3 tablespoons rice vinegar
2 tablespoons shoyu

Mix above ingredients well and pour over somen.

■ KOREAN BARBEQUE SAUCE

1/2 cup sugar
2/3 cup shoyu
3 tablespoons sherry
1/2 teaspoon salt
1 tablespoon toasted
   sesame seeds
1 teaspoon grated ginger
1 clove garlic, grated
2 tablespoons vegetable oil
1 green onion, chopped

Mix above ingredients well; make certain sugar is melted. Marinate chicken, beef, fish, or anything else you want and broil, grill, or fry.

■ SUPER JAPANESE SAUCE

According to Mrs. Nancy Hashimoto, who shared this with me, this recipe came from the former KK Tei, a favorite family-style restaurant known for its jovial host, Mr. KK Kobata. This sauce is good for hekka (stir-fry), nishime (simmered vegetables), pork, and tofu as is any Japanese sugar-shoyu seasoning. If you find the flavor too strong, dilute it with 1/2 cup water.

1 package dashi-no-moto
   (bonito-flavored soup stock)
2 cups shoyu
1 cup mirin
   (sweet rice wine)
1 cup sugar
1/4 cup sake
3 cloves garlic, grated

Cook all ingredients until mixture boils; simmer for 5 minutes. Cool and store in refrigerator for use any time. Use 1/2 cup at a time for any shoyu-sugar seasoning, or more, as needed. Keeps in refrigerator 6 to 8 weeks.

NANA'S SALAD DRESSING

1/4 cup coarsely chopped
   round onion
1 clove garlic, chopped
1/2 cup lime or lemon juice
1/2 teaspoon Colman's
   mustard
1/4 teaspoon Worcestershire
   sauce
3/4 cup sugar
1/4 teaspoon black pepper
2 teaspoons salt
1/2 cup vegetable oil

Mix onion and garlic in blender with lime or lemon juice, mustard, and Worcestershire sauce until liquefied. Add sugar, black pepper, and salt and blend well. Slowly add salad oil and blend well.

■ If added to sugar early, oil will coat sugar and prevent it from blending with remaining ingredients.

MARINARA SAUCE

2 onions, finely chopped
6 tablespoons vegetable oil
1 14.5-ounce can peeled
   tomatoes
1 cup tomato juice
1 teaspoon salt
1 teaspoon sugar
2 teaspoons oregano
1/2 teaspoon basil
1/4 teaspoon black pepper

Sauté onion in oil until transparent. Add canned tomatoes and tomato juice. Season with salt, sugar, oregano, basil, and pepper. Cover and simmer for 20 minutes. Taste and adjust seasonings. If sauce is thin, let it boil down a bit until slightly thickened.

■ TERIYAKI SAUCE

⅓ cup shoyu
¼ cup sugar
½ teaspoon grated garlic
½ teaspoon grated ginger

Mix above ingredients until sugar is melted.
This sauce is good for chicken, beef or fish.

■ PEANUT BUTTER SAUCE for WATERCRESS

2 tablespoons creamy
   peanut butter
1½ tablespoons shoyu
1 tablespoon sugar
1 teaspoon rice vinegar

Mix above ingredients well and pour over
watercress or other cooked green vegetables.
Peanut butter is a more healthful alternative
to miso, which has a lot of sodium.

■ MUSTARD SAUCE for FRESH CORNED BEEF

Fay Lindsey permitted me to share this recipe with you. I use it often and receive positive reviews. You will never use plain mustard for your fresh corned beef again.

½ cup Dijon mustard
½ cup brown sugar
2 tablespoons Colman's mustard
3 tablespoons red wine vinegar
¼ cup salad oil
¼ cup water

Mix all ingredients well.

■ CHERRY-RAISIN HAM GLAZE

1 cup guava jelly
2 tablespoons dark brown sugar
½ teaspoon Colman's mustard
¼ cup sherry
½ cup pineapple juice
¼ cup ketchup
¼ teaspoon cloves
1 cup cherry pie filling
½ cup golden raisins

Mix jelly, brown sugar, mustard, sherry, pineapple juice, ketchup, and cloves; cook until jelly dissolves. Remove 1 cup; add cherry pie filling and golden raisins to remaining mixture. Cook for 10 minutes; set aside.

During last 15 to 20 minutes of baking ham, pour glaze (sans cherries) over ham. Continue baking until done. Pour cherry-raisin glaze over sliced ham before serving.

■SALADS and VEGETABLES

TOFU KIM CHEE SALAD page 39

■ DON'S GRILL'S ROTINI SALAD

Don Hoota was good enough to share this recipe with me many years ago.
He graciously permitted me to share it with you.

1 10-ounce package
   rainbow rotini pasta
1 6-ounce can medium
   olives, sliced
2 6½-ounce jars marinated
   artichoke hearts,
   drained, quartered
3 ounces dry salami slices,
   cut into 6 pieces each
4 ounces smoked ham,
   julienned
4 ounces medium cheddar
   cheese, grated
3 cups bite-size broccoli
   florets
12 ounces Italian dressing

Add pasta to large pot of boiling water.
Stir pasta, cover pot, and turn off burner. Let
covered pot sit on burner for 12 minutes and
then stir, drain, and rinse pasta under running
water; set aside.

Place remaining ingredients except dressing in
a large bowl. Add drained pasta and toss
with dressing.

■ Let cleaned, chopped broccoli sit in a pan
of salted water for 15 minutes. Rinse
and drain. If you prefer broccoli cooked,
microwave it for 2 minutes or longer if desired.

■ GRILLED CHICKEN, SPINACH and CASHEW SALAD

Honey Mustard Dressing

1 teaspoon fresh lemon
   juice
2 tablespoons Dijon mustard
1½ teaspoons ground cumin
2 tablespoons honey
5 tablespoons extra virgin
   olive oil
Salt and pepper to taste

2 boneless chicken breasts
½ teaspoon salt
½ teaspoon freshly ground
   pepper
2 cups baby spinach leaves
½ cup halved cherry
   tomatoes
½ cup roasted, salted
   cashews

In medium bowl combine lemon juice, mustard, cumin, and honey. Pour in olive oil in a steady stream, whisking slowly. Season with salt and pepper; set aside.

Place chicken in a shallow dish with 3 tablespoons dressing. Turn breasts to coat well. Let sit at room temperature for 30 minutes. Grill 4 to 6 minutes on each side. Cut into ½-inch strips.

In large bowl toss spinach, tomatoes, and cashews with remaining dressing. Top with chicken strips when serving.

■ CINNAMON-APPLESAUCE CHEESE SALAD

This recipe is my favorite for Christmas gatherings because it is so colorful. The chopped walnuts and applesauce give it an unusual texture and flavor.

2 3-ounce packages lemon-flavored gelatin
½ cup red cinnamon candy
3 cups boiling water
2 cups applesauce
1 tablespoon lemon juice
⅛ teaspoon salt
½ cup coarsely chopped walnuts
2 3-ounce packages cream cheese, softened with ¼ cup milk
2 tablespoons mayonnaise

Dissolve gelatin and candies in boiling water and stir until candies are thoroughly melted. Stir in applesauce, lemon juice, and salt and chill for 30 minutes in freezer. Add nuts and pour into 9x9-inch pan.

Beat together cream cheese, milk, and mayonnaise and spoon over top of gelatin; cut into gelatin with a spoon and swirl through. Chill until firm and serve.

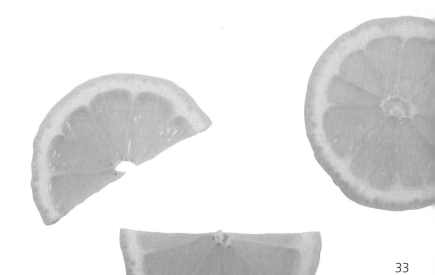

■ MINTY PEAR-CHEESE SALAD

2 3-ounce packages
  lime-flavored gelatin
1/8 teaspoon salt
2 cups boiling water
1 16-ounce can pear halves
6 to 7 drops mint extract
2 3-ounce packages
  cream cheese, softened

Dissolve gelatin and salt in boiling water. Drain pears; measure syrup and add water to make 1³/₄ cups. Stir syrup and mint extract into gelatin. Set aside 1 cup gelatin mixture; pour remainder into 1¹/₂-quart mold. Chill until slightly thickened. Quarter pear halves and place in gelatin. Chill until set but not firm. Gradually blend 1 cup reserved gelatin into cream cheese; pour carefully into pan so mixture sits on top. Chill until firm; unmold and serve. Serves 10.

■ YUM YUM SALAD

2 packages unflavored
  gelatin
1/2 cup water
2 cups crushed pineapple,
  with juice
1/2 cup water
1/2 cup sugar
1 cup cottage cheese
1 bottle Avoset (cream)

Dissolve gelatin in 1/2 cup water and set aside. In pot bring undrained pineapple, 1/2 cup water, and sugar to boil. Take off burner and mix gelatin with pineapple mixture. Cool. Add cottage cheese and unwhipped Avoset; mix well, pour into mold, and refrigerate until firm.

■ SPINACH SALAD

This has always been a favorite of mine and is similar to the warm spinach salads that many restaurants serve.

1 pound fresh spinach
  leaves
2 eggs, boiled, diced
8 slices bacon, crisp and
  broken or ¼ cup
  imitation bacon bits
2 cups fresh bean sprouts
1 8-ounce can sliced water
  chestnuts

Dressing
1 cup oil
⅔ cup sugar
Salt to taste
1 medium onion, grated
¼ cup distilled vinegar
⅓ cup ketchup
1 tablespoon Worcestershire
  sauce

Trim and discard tough spinach stems. Rinse leaves well, pat dry, and break into bite-size pieces in salad bowl. Add remaining ingredients. Mix dressing ingredients together and toss.

■ Leftover dressing keeps well in the refrigerator for at least a week.

■ CHINESE CABBAGE SALAD and DRESSING

1 Chinese cabbage,
  1/2-inch slices
1 package won ton chips

Dressing
1 clove garlic, minced
1 cup vegetable oil
1/2 cup sugar
1/2 cup distilled vinegar
2 teaspoons salt
1/2 teaspoon black pepper
1/4 cup mayonnaise
1 teaspoon dry mustard

Mix dressing ingredients and toss with cabbage. Garnish with won ton chips.

■ BROCCOLI-CRAB SALAD

1 large broccoli head
1/4 cup raisins
1/3 cup artificial crab, chopped
2 tablespoons mayonnaise or
  vegenaise ■
1 tablespoon sugar
1 tablespoon distilled vinegar

Clean broccoli, chop into bite-size pieces, and microwave for 1 1/2 minutes. Cool. Add raisins and chopped artificial crab. Mix mayonnaise or vegenaise, sugar, and vinegar. Toss with broccoli.

■ As a substitute for mayonnaise, use Follow Your Heart grape seed oil vegenaise, which is available at health food stores. Your heart will thank you.

■ SHIRA AE

While growing up, I turned up my nose at "old folks' food," but as I grow older, I notice that my tastes change. Others tell me they also notice this trend in themselves.

1 bunch watercress or
   spinach
2 to 3 tablespoons shoyu
1 block firm tofu
1 carton shirataki
   (konnyaku■ strips)
1/2 teaspoon salt
2 tablespoons sesame seeds
3 tablespoons miso
2 tablespoons sugar

Wash and boil watercress or spinach. Drain greens, squeeze out water, and cut into 1-inch pieces; sprinkle with shoyu and set aside. Boil quartered tofu in water for 5 minutes, drain, and squeeze dry. Cut drained shirataki into 1/2-inch pieces; fry in a nonstick pan with 1/2 teaspoon salt; stir constantly until dry. Toast sesame seeds in small covered pan over medium heat until seeds start popping and turn light brown. Shake pan to keep seeds from burning.

Grind sesame seeds in suribachi (mortar)■ until finely ground. Add miso and sugar; continue mixing in suribachi/mortar. Add tofu and continue mixing. Add seasoned shirataki and watercress. Refrigerate.

■ Konnyaku is a translucent, gelatin-like product made from a type of potato. It absorbs the flavors of dishes with which it is cooked.

■ The *Honolulu Advertiser* describes a suribachi as a bowl with rows of narrow grooves etched into an unfinished ceramic interior, perfect for grinding sesame seeds. The pestle looks like a short, tapered rolling pin without the handles. The back of a large wooden spoon works as well.

■ Leftovers keep well in the refrigerator. Boiling the tofu helps preserve it, and squeezing it dry prevents water from diluting the taste.

■ COLESLAW

½ medium cabbage,
   finely shredded
2 tablespoons sugar
2 tablespoons rice vinegar
¼ teaspoon salt
¼ teaspoon yellow mustard
2 tablespoons mayonnaise

Combine ingredients and refrigerate until ready to serve.

■ COLESLAW SAIMIN SALAD

3 tablespoons butter
½ cup slivered almonds
⅓ cup sesame seeds
2 packages raw saimin, crushed
1 medium cabbage, shredded

Dressing
½ cup oil
¼ cup sugar
¼ cup white wine vinegar
2 tablespoons shoyu
Pepper to taste

Melt butter, add almonds, sesame seeds, and crushed saimin. Brown and cool. Toss with cabbage and dressing.

■ TOFU KIM CHEE SALAD

1 block firm tofu, drained
2 eggs
1 tablespoon water
2 sheets nori
1 cup kim chee, finely
    chopped
2 tablespoons chopped
    green onion
1 teaspoon sesame seeds

Sauce
1 small chili pepper, seeded
½ teaspoon sesame oil
3 tablespoons shoyu
Dash black pepper

Cut tofu into bite-size pieces.
Mix eggs with 1 tablespoon
water; fry eggs into thin sheets
and slice. Crisp nori over burner.

Place tofu in serving dish. Top
with chopped kim chee, sliced
egg, and slivered nori. Pour
sauce over and garnish with
green onion and sesame seeds.

■ BROCCOLI SALAD

Men usually don't like raisins in a salad, but to my surprise, the men who have eaten this salad like it.

3 cups broccoli florets
  and stems
½ cup raisins
½ cup thinly sliced
  red onion
1/2 cup bacon bits
1 cup broken cashew nuts

Dressing
¾ cup mayonnaise
¼ cup sugar
2 tablespoons distilled
  vinegar

Chop broccoli florets and stems into bite-size pieces. Toss with remaining ingredients except nuts; cover and refrigerate for 1 hour before serving. Combine dressing ingredients and toss with nuts before serving.

■ Though the recipe calls for raw broccoli, you may blanch the florets if you prefer.

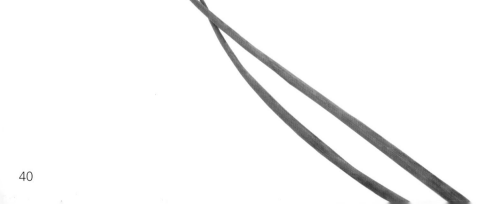

■ POTATO-MACARONI SALAD

My deceased sister-in-law, Fumi, made the most wonderful potato-macaroni salad; this is my attempt at imitating hers. I put this recipe together when our son Daryl called from California asking for it. After he had made it, he called to say I had not told him how much this recipe made. He has since reduced it to a manageable quantity.

4 large potatoes

2 cups macaroni

6 large eggs, boiled

White pepper to taste

2½ teaspoons salt, divided

2¼ teaspoons sugar, divided

1 cup frozen peas, cooked, drained

1 large sweet onion, grated, drained

½ cup coarsely grated carrots

1 cup mayonnaise

Wash potatoes, wipe dry, and punch 10 to 12 holes over face of each potato. Microwave 2 at a time, 5 minutes on one side and another 5 to 6 minutes on other side. Seal in foil and let sit for 15 minutes. Peel and refrigerate overnight.

In a large pot bring 12 cups water to a rapid boil. Add macaroni, stir, replace cover, and turn off burner. Let covered pot sit on burner for 20 minutes. Stir macaroni, which will be lumped together, rinse, and drain well.

Boil eggs in pan lined with a paper towel to prevent eggs from banging around as they cook. Cook on medium heat for 13 to 14 minutes, making certain that last 1 minute is at full boil. Remove pot from burner. Let covered pot sit for 15 minutes. Drain, cool, peel, and chop eggs coarsely. (See *Cooking and Household Tips* for best way to boil eggs.)

Chop potatoes and season with a dash of white pepper and ½ teaspoon each salt and sugar. Add drained macaroni, mix, and add another ¼ teaspoon each salt and sugar and dash of white pepper. Add chopped eggs and remaining ingredients. Add 1¾ teaspoons salt and 1½ teaspoons sugar, and dash of white pepper. Taste. Add more seasonings if desired. You should be able to taste the onion slightly. If you do not, add more grated onion or onion powder to taste. (I believe the onion was Fumi's secret ingredient.) Chill thoroughly before serving. Serves 20.

■ SWEET POTATO SALAD

This is one of my favorite salads from Mrs. Hamada, who shared many recipes with her fellow sewing students during mid-morning break. I strongly suspect that the break, when we shared snacks as well as recipes, was what motivated us to keep returning to class. Of course, Mrs. Abe probably had something to do with it as well; she was a wonderful, talented instructor who taught us how to make many beautiful muumuus and outfits.

3 large boiled Okinawan
   sweet potatoes
1 cup chopped celery
3/4 cup chopped
   (1/2-inch cubes) red onion
3/4 cup chopped (1/2-inch
   cubes) green pepper
3/4 cup chopped (1/2-inch
   cubes) red bell pepper
3/4 cup chopped (1/2-inch
   cubes) yellow pepper

Dressing
1/4 red onion, coarsely
chopped
1 clove garlic, chopped
1/2 cup rice vinegar
3/4 cup sugar
2 teaspoons salt
1/4 teaspoon white pepper
1/4 teaspoon Worcestershire
   sauce
1 bay leaf, crushed
1/2 teaspoon mustard
1 cup vegetable oil

Boil potatoes the day before; peel and chill overnight, a process that firms the flesh and keeps potatoes from getting mashed when tossed with other ingredients. Chop potatoes into 1/2-inch cubes. Combine with vegetables.

To make dressing, blend onion and garlic in blender and add remaining ingredients, adding oil last. Pour over potatoes and vegetables and gently fold to mix.

■ SWEET POTATO and PEAS SALAD

I tasted this at a graduation party and found it refreshingly different.

4 medium Okinawa sweet
   potatoes
1 cup frozen peas
½ cup chopped red onion
1 teaspoon salt
¼ teaspoon white pepper
1 cup raisins
1 cup mayonnaise

Boil sweet potatoes the night before and refrigerate. The next day, slice and dice potatoes into bite-size pieces. Add peas to pot of boiling water. Turn off burner; let peas sit for 5 minutes and drain.

Mix all ingredients and refrigerate until ready to serve.

VEGETABLES

■ SESAME BROCCOLI

1 large broccoli head
1/3 cup sesame seeds, toasted
1 1/2 tablespoons soy sauce
2 teaspoons sesame oil
2 teaspoons honey
2 teaspoons sugar
1 tablespoon miso

Peel broccoli, cut into florets, and cook in boiling salted water until tender-crisp. Drain thoroughly and let cool to room temperature. Combine remaining ingredients in large bowl. Shortly before serving, add broccoli and toss to mix well. Serves 6. .

■ GREEN BEANS WITH MISO SAUCE

Marge Torigoe gave me this recipe, which is a good standby when you want a cooked vegetable.

1 pound green beans
3 cups water

Sauce
1/3 cup mayonnaise
2 1/2 tablespoons miso
1 1/2 tablespoons sugar

Cut beans into 1-inch pieces; bring water to boil and simmer beans until tender, about 15 to 20 minutes. Drain and cool. Mix sauce ingredients, pour over beans, and mix lightly. Chill for 1 hour before serving. Serves 6.

■ MISO YAKI BITTER MELON

2 cups slivered bitter melon
2 tablespoons tiny dried
   shrimp
1 tablespoon vegetable oil
4 tablespoons miso
3 tablespoons sugar
1 tablespoon shoyu
1 tablespoon sesame seed

Wash and cut bitter melon in half lengthwise. Scrape out seeds and cut into slanted 1/4-inch slivers. Set aside. Fry shrimp in hot oil for 1 minute. Add miso, sugar, shoyu, and sesame seeds and mix well. Add slivered bitter melon and cook for another 1 to 2 minutes, stirring constantly to prevent burning. Do not over-cook bitter melon.

Note: If you are like me and do not care for bitter melon, you might hesitate to try this recipe. My recollection of bitter melon from my childhood was that it was BITTER. If not overcooked, it is actually slightly sweet. Try it; you might like it.

■ GREEN BEAN CASSEROLE

I made this a couple of years ago for our Thanksgiving gathering in Laguna Niguel. It is easy to prepare and quite good.

2 10-ounce packages frozen French-style cut green beans, cooked, drained
1 10¾-ounce can mushroom soup
1 tablespoon soy sauce
Dash pepper
1 3.5-ounce can French fried onion rings

Cook beans as directed and drain. Preheat oven to 350 degrees. In 1-quart casserole, combine soup, soy sauce, and pepper; mix well. Stir in green beans and 1½ cups onion rings. Bake for 20 minutes. Top with remaining rings and bake another 5 minutes. Serves 6.

■ KOREAN GREEN BEANS

2 tablespoons vegetable oil
¼ pound beef or chicken, thinly sliced
1 onion, thinly sliced
½ cup sliced mushrooms
1 10-ounce package frozen French-style green beans, thawed
1 clove garlic, minced
½ cup water
1 tablespoon soy sauce
1 beef bouillon cube, crushed
Salt and freshly ground pepper

Heat oil in large skillet over medium-high heat. Add beef or chicken and sauté until browned, about 2 minutes. Stir in onion and mushrooms and cook another 2 to 3 minutes. Add beans and stir-fry 1 minute. Blend in garlic, water, soy sauce, and bouillon. Cover and continue cooking until beans are tender and mixture is heated through, about 5 to 7 minutes. Season with salt and pepper. Serve over rice. Serves 6.

■ SOUTHERN CORN PUDDING

Thank you Doris Sugihara for sharing this recipe with me. She and the other women who worked with me at the police department readily shared recipes with each other.

2 eggs
1 14-ounce can creamed
   corn
1 tablespoon sugar
2 tablespoons butter or
   margarine, melted
½ cup milk
1 teaspoon salt
⅛ teaspoon white pepper

Beat eggs to combine yolks and whites; add remaining ingredients. Mix well and pour into greased 1½-quart baking dish; set dish in pan of hot water and bake at 350 degrees for an hour. Serves 6

■ FRIED PEPPERED CABBAGE

1 medium head cabbage
4 tablespoons butter
Salt and pepper to taste
3 tablespoons sour cream

Wash cabbage, remove core, and chop coarsely. Melt butter in large skillet over high heat. Add cabbage and sauté, stirring constantly, until cabbage is tender-crisp, about 2 minutes. (It should not be wilted or cooked through.) Season with salt and a very generous amount of pepper. Stir in sour cream and serve immediately.

■ CAULIFLOWER WITH CAPER SAUCE

This is a unique dish that will elicit compliments. You will serve this easy-to-prepare dish often.

1 large cauliflower head
1 tablespoon cornstarch
1 tablespoon water
3 tablespoons butter
1 tablespoon fresh
   lemon juice
1 tablespoon grated onion
¼ teaspoon salt
⅛ teaspoon freshly
   ground black pepper
1 teaspoon turmeric
2 tablespoons capers

Place cauliflower in 1 inch boiling salted water. Cover and cook for 15 minutes. Remove cauliflower to warm serving dish; cover with foil to keep warm.

Reserve 1 cup cooking liquid. Soften cornstarch in 1 tablespoon water and blend into reserved cooking liquid, stirring constantly. Add butter, lemon juice, onion, salt, pepper, and turmeric. Cook, stirring until sauce thickens. Remove from heat, stir in capers, and pour over cauliflower.

■ Turmeric turns plastic utensils and plates yellow. It washes off gradually, but when possible, use metal utensils.

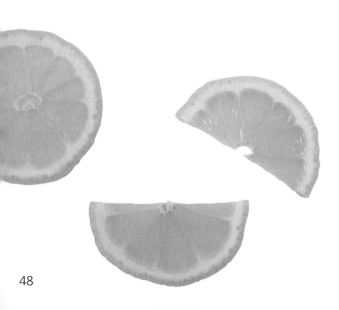

■ CHINESE PICKLED MUSTARD CABBAGE, TURNIPS, or CARROTS

Keeps well in the refrigerator so prepare more than you need for one recipe and keep in the refrigerator for several weeks.

2 large heads mustard
  cabbage, OR
1 pound turnips, sliced, OR
1 pound carrots, sliced
4 tablespoons sugar
4 tablespoons rice vinegar
1 tablespoon cornstarch
1/3 cup water

Blanch sliced vegetables in boiling salted water and rinse in cold water. Boil carrots for 3 minutes; boil mustard cabbage or turnips for 2 minutes. Drain water from cabbage.

Gently boil sugar and vinegar for 5 minutes. Cool. Add vegetables to vinegar mixture and chill for one day.

Slice and add to cooked beef or chicken for a sweet-sour dish. Thicken with 1 tablespoon cornstarch mixed with 1/3 cup water.

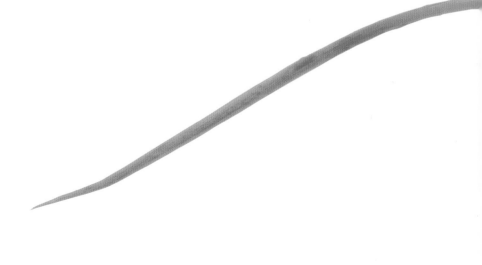

SUSHI and RICE

ROAST BEEF & PICKLES ROLL page 60

MATSUTAKE MESHI
(MUSHROOM RICE)

2 cups uncooked
   Calrose rice
2 tablespoons sake
1 cup canned sliced
   mushrooms
6 tablespoons mushroom
   liquid
¼ cup shiitake mushrooms,
   soaked, slivered
1 tablespoon shoyu
¼ teaspoon salt
2 cups water

Wash rice and drain. Place in bottom of ungreased baking dish and add mushrooms.

In separate pan mix all other ingredients and bring to a boil. Add to rice and mushrooms. Cover and bake at 350 degrees for 40 minutes. Serves 6.

■ TORI MESHI (CHICKEN RICE)

2 cups uncooked
   Calrose rice
4 shiitake mushrooms,
   soaked
5 boneless, skinless chicken
   thighs
½ cup chopped carrots
½ cup chopped gobo
   (burdock)
2½ cups water
2 tablespoons soy sauce
2 tablespoons sake
1½ teaspoons salt
1 teaspoon dashi-no-moto
   (bonito-flavored soup
   stock)
Dashi konbu
   (dried seaweed)

Cut carrots and gobo into thin diagonal slices. Cut slices into ⅛-inch slivers. Set aside. Rinse and drain rice. Remove stems from mushrooms and cut caps into thin strips. In rice pot combine all ingredients except dashi konbu. Mix well. Place a piece of dashi konbu on top of rice for added flavor. Cover tightly and cook until done.

■ When you're in a hurry, this is a great "dinner in a rice bowl." Adjust seasonings according to taste the second time around.

■ BEST FRIED RICE

6 strips bacon
½ cup chopped round onion
¼ teaspoon salt
1 tablespoon shoyu
½ cup chopped ham
4 cups cooked Calrose rice
3 tablespoons shoyu
1 egg, beaten
1 teaspoon water
Pinch salt
3 tablespoons chopped
   green onion

Cut bacon into 1/8-inch pieces and fry until almost crisp. Drain fat, add round onion, and continue cooking until onion is cooked. Add ¼ teaspoon salt and 1 tablespoon shoyu; mix well. Add ham and cooked rice; continue stirring until each grain of rice is separated. Add shoyu and stir to coat rice evenly. Beat egg, water, and salt and fry into a thin layer in a hot skillet; sliver or chop egg into ¼-inch pieces. Add egg pieces and chopped green onion to rice and adjust seasonings to taste.

■ THAI FRIED RICE

This is exactly the way the Thai restaurants prepare their fried rice.
It's good, yet simple.

2 tablespoons vegetable oil
8 ounces large (21 to 30 per
   pound) shrimp, deveined
1 clove garlic, chopped
1 egg
3 ounces pineapple chunks,
   drained
1 tablespoon soy sauce
½ teaspoon ketchup
⅓ teaspoon sugar
⅛ teaspoon white pepper
2 cups cooked, cooled
   Calrose rice

Heat oil in large skillet. Add shrimp and garlic; stir-fry until garlic is lightly browned, about 1 minute. Move to side of pan and add 1 beaten egg to scramble in pan. Add seasonings and stir-fry until shrimp is thoroughly cooked, about 2 minutes.

■ BROILED SUSHI

9 shiitake mushrooms,
   soaked, finely chopped
10 sticks imitation crab,
   chopped
1 cup sour cream
1 cup mayonnaise
4 cups cooked, cooled
Calrose rice
Furikake (prepared sesame
   seed and seaweed)
Korean nori

Mix shiitake, crabmeat, sour cream, and mayonnaise. Spread cooled, cooked rice in bottom of 9x13-inch baking pan. Sprinkle furikake over rice. Spread crab mixture over layer of furikake and broil for 6 to 8 minutes until mixture starts to brown nicely. Cool and cut into 24 pieces. Wrap each piece of rice in a piece of Korean nori and serve.

■ LAYERED SUSHI RICE with CRAB and TAKUAN

1 package imitation crab,
  chopped
1½ cups mayonnaise
Furikake (prepared sesame
   seed and seaweed)
3 cups cooked, cooled
   Calrose rice
1 Japanese cucumber,
   thinly sliced
1 long takuan (pickled
   daikon, or Chinese
   radish), thinly sliced

Mix chopped imitation crab with mayonnaise. Liberally sprinkle furikake in bottom of baking pan. Pack cooled rice over furikake and spread crab mixture over it. Layer cucumber and then takuan over crab. Sprinkle with more furikake and then cover with plastic wrap. Press down to pack toppings. Cut and serve.

■ SEKIHAN

1 8-ounce package azuki
   beans
3 cups mochi (also known as
   sweet) rice
1 cup uncooked Calrose rice
2 tablespoons sake
1 teaspoon salt

Soak azuki beans overnight in 5 cups water. Add salt and cook beans 30 to 40 minutes. Do not overcook beans. Save liquid.

Combine mochi rice and Calrose rice, wash, and soak for 30 minutes or more before cooking. Drain washed rice. Measure azuki liquid and add water to equal 4 cups liquid. Mix liquid with azuki, rice, and sake. Stir. Cook in rice cooker until rice is cooked. Serve with Goma Jio (recipe follows).

■ GOMA JIO (SESAME SALT)

3 tablespoons toasted
   black sesame seeds
1 tablespoon salt

Pan-broil sesame seeds and salt, stirring constantly until heated. Use over Sekihan and other rice dishes.

6 cups uncooked
 Calrose rice
6 cups water
2 teaspoons salt
³/₄ cup sugar, less
 1 tablespoon
³/₄ cup Mitsukan rice
 vinegar
2 aburage (fried tofu),
 finely chopped
¹/₄ cup vegetable oil
1 medium carrot, grated
¹/₄ cup sugar
¹/₄ cup shoyu
1 6-ounce can ajitsuke
 kogai (seasoned
 baby clams)
1 6-ounce stick kamabuko
 (fish cake), julienned
1 1.5-ounce package
 kurome (dried seaweed),
 washed, soaked, drained,
 chopped

Wash rice and cook in 6 cups water. Let steam 10 to 20 minutes.

Add vinegar, salt, and sugar to blender container and blend for 2 minutes until sugar and salt have completely dissolved. Set aside and let sit until sauce is clear.

Cook chopped aburage in oil until crisp. Add grated carrot and cook 2 minutes. Add sugar and shoyu and when boiling add ajitsuke kogai, kamabuko, and kurome. Cook another 2 minutes.

When rice has finished steaming, place in a nonmetallic container. Add vinegar sauce and mix well to coat each grain of rice. Add vegetable mixture and mix well. Serve warm or cold.

■ This is an excellent potluck dish. Leftovers keep well in the refrigerator and can be eaten cold.

■ INARI SUSHI (CONE SUSHI)

12 large or 24 small
    aburage (fried tofu)
2½ cups water
¼ cup dried shrimp,
    shredded
4 tablespoons shoyu
¾ teaspoon salt
6 tablespoons sugar
1 package dashi-no-moto
    (bonito-flavored soup
    stock)
1 carrot, chopped
String beans, chopped

Cut aburage in half and rinse in hot tap water 3 times to remove the oil in which it was fried. Carefully peel open each half; squeeze dry and place in pot with 2½ cups water and seasonings. Cook for 30 minutes. As aburage float to the surface, gently push them down. They tear easily, so remove them carefully from pot; drain, reserving liquid, and cool.

Reserve the liquid for the gu (filling). Add dashi-no-moto, carrot, and beans; cook until tender. Add drained cooked vegetables and shredded shrimp to Sushi Rice (page 58); mix well and fill aburage.

TEMAKI SUSHI
Hand-Rolled Sushi

■ SUSHI RICE

Use this rice for any type of seasoned sushi

6 cups uncooked Calrose rice
6 cups water

Basic Sushi Vinegar
1 cup + 2 tablespoons sugar
$2/3$ cup Mitsukan or other
   Japanese rice vinegar
2 tablespoons salt

Wash rice and drain well; add 6 cups water and let stand for 30 minutes before cooking. After rice is cooked, let it sit for 20 to 30 minutes. (Rice used immediately after cooking will be mushy and extra moist.) Place cooked rice in a nonmetal container. Place sugar, vinegar, and salt in a blender container and blend until salt and sugar are completely dissolved. Let sit until mixture is clear, about 10 minutes. Pour over cooled rice and mix gently until mixture coats every particle of rice. You are now ready to use it for any type of seasoned sushi.

■ **Wraps:** For variety, use red or green lettuce leaves in place of nori to wrap sushi. Nori is not available in some places or is a foreign taste to others, so be creative. Use anything that will hold rice and fillings together.

■ **Fillings:** I have used egg salad with julienned cucumbers and avocado to imitate California sushi. Julienned zucchini, takuan (pickled daikon, or Chinese radish), and kamabuko (fish cake) also work well; the possibilities are limited only by your imagination.

4 spears asparagus

4 small dill or sweet pickles

1 12-ounce can corned beef, flaked

4 sheets thin omelet (recipe follows)

3 cups cooked Sushi Rice (page 58)

Cook asparagus in salted water until crisp-tender, about 5 minutes. Drain and set aside. Cut pickles lengthwise into quarters. Flake corned beef. Place plastic wrap on bamboo mat. Lay one thin omelet sheet on top and spread evenly with 3/4 cup rice. Place 1/4 of corned beef, 1 asparagus spear, and 4 pickle quarters in center of rice. To roll omelet, press lightly and lift mat as you roll toward opposite end. Roll, pressing firmly. Repeat with remaining ingredients. Remove mat. Cut and serve.

Thin Omelet Roll

1 1/3 tablespoons cornstarch

1 1/3 tablespoons water

1 teaspoon salt

4 large eggs, beaten

Vegetable oil for frying

Mix cornstarch, water, and salt. Add to beaten eggs. Spray nonstick pan with cooking spray. Place over medium heat. Pour in just enough egg mixture to cover bottom of skillet. Rotate skillet to distribute egg evenly. Omelet is ready when edges curl up and surface becomes glossy. Slide out onto waxed paper or plastic wrap. Omelet should be tissue thin. Place waxed paper or plastic wrap between each omelet.

■ ROAST BEEF and PICKLES ROLL

12 slices roast beef
12 leaves red leaf lettuce
1/4 cup horseradish sauce
12 pickle slices
    (cut lengthwise)
Sushi Rice (page 58)

Place 1 slice roast beef on lettuce leaf and top with 1 teaspoon horseradish. Add 1 sliver of pickle and top with 3 tablespoons Sushi Rice. Fold bottom of lettuce leaf over and fold both sides toward center.

■ HAWAIIAN ROLL

8 slices canned pineapple
½ pound ham, julienned
Sushi Rice (page 58)
Red leaf lettuce

Cut each pineapple slice into 8 pieces. Cut ham into ¼-inch slices. Place 2 to 3 tablespoons rice on lettuce leaf, and place 1 slice ham and 1 or more pineapple pieces in center. Fold up bottom of leaf and then fold both sides toward center.

■ SUSHI MAYO SAUCE

This is an excellent sauce for any type of sushi.

1 cup mayonnaise
4 teaspoons honey
4 teaspoons sesame seeds
1 1/2 teaspoons sesame oil

Mix well and enjoy.

■ CHICKEN TERIYAKI ROLL

1/2 pound boneless chicken
    breast, julienned
1/2 cup teriyaki sauce
3 tablespoons toasted
    sesame seeds
1 T. salt
Red leaf lettuce
Clover sprouts
Sushi Rice (page 58)

Soak strips of chicken in teriyaki sauce for 1 hour. Mix together sesame seeds and salt. Broil or grill chicken until cooked through. Cool. Place 1 piece of chicken on each lettuce leaf. Add clover sprouts to taste and sprinkle with toasted sesame seed–and-salt mixture. Top with 3 tablespoons sushi rice, fold up bottom of leaf, and fold both sides toward center.

In the 1960s I tasted Mrs. Seichi Mukai's Tokyo-style sushi (the big fat ones with lots of gu) and dreamed about duplicating it. It took me years of experimentation; the following recipe is the result. You have to try it at least once because this is the best sushi ever. You may reduce the number of gu (fillings) if you desire.

Sushi Rice (page 58)

Gu (Filling)

1/2 cup washed raw sugar
1/4 cup shoyu
1/4 cup sherry
1 teaspoon salt
1 cup water
3-ounce package kampyo
     (dried gourd strips)
1 package (10 sheets) nori
8 8 1/2-inch strips gobo,
     peeled, soaked, and cut
     into strips (cut thick
     strips into halves or
     quarters)
15 large shiitake mushrooms,
     soaked and softened in
     warm water for 2 to 3
     hours
12 to 16 long string beans
8 large eggs
3 6-ounce cans tuna

Bring washed raw sugar, shoyu, sherry, salt, and water to a boil in a covered pot large enough to cook the following, layered in order:

■ **Kampyo:** Moisten and rub with 2 tablespoons salt; rinse and soak in warm water for 3 to 4 hours. Measure and cut kampyo to length of nori. If kampyo is thin, measure it 3 times the length; if thick, 2.

■ **Gobo:** Peel, soak, and cut into 12 strips the length of the nori. If thick, cut into halves or quarters.

■ **Carrots:** Peel 1 large carrot; slice into 12 strips 1/2-inch thick and slightly longer than the nori; carrot strips will shrink when cooked.

■ **Shiitake mushrooms:** Soak and soften in warm water for 2 to 3 hours.

Cover pot and bring to boiling over medium heat; boil for 10 minutes; remove carrots. Continue cooking another 10 minutes; turn off heat and leave pan on burner, covered, for another 30 minutes. Remove shiitake, squeeze out excess sauce, and cut into 1/4-inch strips. Drain remaining ingredients and lay them in a row on a large baking sheet, starting with sliced mushrooms and ending with kampyo. Laying them out this way will ensure that you will not miss any ingredients.

■ **Long string beans:** If beans are thick, cut in half lengthwise before cooking. Boil in water with 2 tablespoons salt for 8 minutes. Drain and cool.

■ **Eggs:** Beat eggs with 1 tablespoon water and $\frac{1}{4}$ teaspoon salt. Fry in lightly oiled hot pan. After 1 minute, lower heat to medium; cover with foil and continue cooking another minute. Remove pan from burner and let sit for 1 to 2 minutes, checking to see that eggs continue cooking but are not puffing up or turning gray. (This will take some practice. Don't give up. Egg should be yellow and barely cooked.) Slice into 12 strips $\frac{1}{2}$-inch thick.

■ **Tuna:** Drain tuna, mash, and cook in small saucepan with 2 tablespoons washed raw sugar, $\frac{1}{3}$ cup shoyu, and $\frac{1}{4}$ teaspoon powdered ginger. Cook 5 to 6 minutes until shoyu has been absorbed and mixture is semi-dry. Set aside in 2 bowls until ready to use. You will have enough tuna in one bowl for 5 rolls of sushi.

Place bamboo sushi mat on your working surface with string binding the mat running perpendicular to you. Put nori on mat shiny side down. Place one tightly packed cup of rice on bottom half of nori and spread rice gently with your fingers to cover $\frac{3}{4}$ of nori, slightly building up outer edges, leaving about an inch of nori free of rice at top. Starting with some tuna, place your ingredients across middle of rice field. Add mushrooms and continue until all seven ingredients have been placed on rice, ending with kampyo.

Pick up bottom ends of nori and mat and fold them over ingredients, while continuing to roll. Tuck in nori only under ingredients and continue to roll firmly while pushing top end of bamboo mat straight out, parallel to bottom of mat, until you have rolled sushi almost completely off the opposite end of mat. Continue rolling sushi. Re-roll mat over completed sushi and gently squeeze sushi to make it firm. While holding sushi in your left hand, push protruding sushi rice at both ends back into sushi. Unroll it from mat and lay it on a surface lined with waxed paper and continue rolling. You should be able to make 10 maki sushis from this recipe.

If you like unagi, you can use 2 cans of Hanamako unagi and a cheaper brand of teriyaki mackerel, mashed together, in place of seasoned tuna.

HAWAIIAN
FAVORITES

■ SQUID LUAU

Atsushi Sato is our favorite squid luau chef. I got this recipe by watching him prepare it for our family. My son-in-law, Rick, loves this dish, providing I cut back on the coconut milk. I use less when making it for him.

1 pound calamari squid
3 2-inch slices ginger
1 package frozen luau leaf
   or 2 bags fresh luau leaf,
   cooked■
1½ to 2 12-ounce cans
   Mendonca's coconut milk

Slit open squid by inserting a paring knife into edge facing you. Remove innards. Cut head from rest of body just above eyes. Cut squid skin in half and slice crosswise into ½-inch slices. If legs are large, cut into several smaller chunks.

Cook sliced squid with ginger in saucepan on medium-low heat. If liquid from squid evaporates, add just enough water to keep squid from burning. Cook until squid is soft, 45 minutes to 1 hour. Remove ginger and set squid aside.

When ready to serve, add drained luau leaf and bring to boil. (If using fresh luau leaf, see directions below.) Add coconut milk and let it come to boil again. Stir to prevent burning. (Use a wooden spoon when preparing this dish. Do not reuse the spoon used for tasting. The coconut milk will turn sour if you do.) You may add a little sugar, but the coconut milk is probably sufficiently sweet.

Lower heat and continue cooking and mixing until luau leaf looks like mushy canned spinach. Drain. A portion can be frozen at this stage if you have more than you need.

■ Wash fresh luau leaves and cook in a large pot over medium heat with ½ inch water. Tear several handfuls and cook until leaves wilt. Add more leaves and spoon cooked portion on top. Continue to add more handfuls until all leaves are cooked. Stir to prevent burning. If liquid cooks down, add ½ cup water. (If heat is not too high, this probably will not be necessary, as water is expressed from leaves while they cook.)

■ CHICKEN LONG RICE

Esther Kekuna always made chicken long rice for our gatherings. She learned it from her niece Leilani Thompson of Kona, who made the best long rice ever.

1 7.75-ounce package Wing
    long rice (bean threads)
2 pounds boneless, skinless
    chicken thighs
1 tablespoon Hawaiian salt
2-inch piece ginger, sliced
2 green onions, chopped

Soak long rice for 2 hours in 6 cups hot tap water. Drain and cut into 6-inch pieces. Place chicken, salt, and ginger in pan with water to cover and boil for 25 to 30 minutes. Reserve chicken broth. Cool chicken and shred into bite-size pieces.

Cook long rice in reserved chicken broth until translucent and soft, 6 to 8 minutes. Add shredded chicken and taste. Add more salt if needed. Add a can of chicken broth if liquid is absorbed by long rice while sitting. Top with chopped green onion just before serving.

■ LUAU STEW

1 tablespoon Hawaiian salt
1½ pounds boneless
    stew meat
1 tablespoon vegetable oil
5 1-inch slices ginger
4 cloves garlic, crushed
4 to 5 cups water
5 to 6 pounds luau leaf

Salt meat and brown in hot oil with ginger and garlic. When nicely browned, add water and cook until meat softens, about 1 hour.

Wash leaves and tear into pieces. Add one large handful at a time to meat. Cook until leaves wilt. Turn meat over and add remaining leaves. Continue cooking, making certain that there is enough liquid to prevent burning; add more water as needed. Continue to turn leaves and meat. Simmer until leaves are soft and have no bitter aftertaste. Add more salt if needed. Discard ginger and garlic and serve.

■ OVEN-BAKED KĀLUA PIG

Now you can prepare your own authentic Hawaiian luau. This recipe is included thanks to the Satos and Kekunas, who are the best in my book when it comes to preparing Hawaiian food.

4 ti leaves, deveined
  (rib stripped off)
4 to 5 pounds pork shoulder
  butt, thawed
⅓ 3.5-ounce bottle Wright's
  liquid smoke
⅓ to ½ cup Hawaiian salt

Place 28x18-inch piece heavy-duty aluminum foil on working area so length runs parallel to working surface. Lay 2 ti leaves, side by side, lengthwise on top of foil. Lay 2 more ti leaves, side by side, on top of and perpendicular to first two. Place pork butt in center and wipe it dry. Pour ⅓ bottle liquid smoke over top and sides. Sprinkle top and sides with Hawaiian salt.

Fold ends of ti leaves toward center. Hold them down and seal foil. To seal, pull together two ends of foil and fold them down as many times as needed to seal pork tightly. To prevent leakage, fold open ends twice.

Place sealed pork in baking pan and bake in oven at 450 degrees for 4 hours. After meat has cooled for 3 hours, pull it off bone with tongs and let it cool off enough to shred further. Bag and refrigerate or freeze it.

When ready to serve, place shredded pork in pot with ½ cup water. If you need more seasoning, add ½ tablespoon rock salt and mix while heating. Cover with foil to keep warm.

■ HAWAIIAN POKE

This recipe is similar to an Oriental shoyu poke. You can omit the shoyu, sesame oil, and ginger for an authentic Hawaiian poke. Keep it refrigerated until ready to serve.

2 pounds 'ahi
1 medium sweet round
   onion
1/2 tablespoon Hawaiian
   salt
6 green onions
Shoyu to taste
1/2 teaspoon sesame seed
   oil (optional)
2 to 3 teaspoons grated
   ginger (optional)

Cut fish into 1/2-inch cubes. Slice round onion into thin slices and then into 1-inch pieces. Chop green onions into 1/4-inch pieces.

In a medium bowl place layer of fish. Sprinkle with 1/2 teaspoon salt and add layer of round onion. Repeat until fish and onion are used up. Top with sliced green onions. Add 1/2 teaspoon sesame oil and mix thoroughly. If desired, add grated ginger to provide the zip that is lacking in some poke.

Marinate fish in refrigerator half a day.

■ You can buy pre-packaged 'ahi from Thailand in 1-pound plastic bags. The fish comes treated with a preservative so it retains its "fresh" color. Noh makes a poke mix in 0.4-ounce packages, the right amount for this quantity of fish, and you get perfect poke every time.

■ LOMI SALMON

¼ pound salted salmon,
   soaked, diced
3 medium tomatoes, diced
2 green onions, sliced
1 small round onion, thinly
   sliced and then diced

Rinse salted salmon 3 times, cover with water, and soak for 3 to 4 hours, changing water often. Remove bones, slice into ½-inch strips, and dice. If you find salmon too salty, squeeze liquid from salmon and reserve to add later with remaining ingredients (if you think it needs more salt at that stage).

Dice tomatoes and lomi (mix/mash) it with salmon. Add green onions and round onions. Mix well. Refrigerate until ready to serve. If finished dish does not have enough liquid, you can add some ice cubes.

■ Our good friend Atsushi, who prepares the best lomi salmon, adds 1 14.5-ounce can diced tomatoes, which gives the dish a little zip and a lot of color.

■ CHICKEN

SKEWERED PEANUT BUTTER CHICKEN page 75

■ CANTONESE CHICKEN

5 pounds boneless chicken
   thighs
1/4 cup soy sauce
1/4 cup lemon juice
1/2 cup ketchup
1/4 cup honey
1-inch piece ginger, crushed

Arrange chicken in baking pan. Combine remaining ingredients and pour over chicken. Bake at 350 degrees until chicken is tender, about 1 hour. Serves 6.

■ STEAMED CHICKEN

1 pound chicken breasts
2 shiitake mushrooms,
   soaked and sliced
1 green onion, diced

Marinade
2 teaspoons peanut oil
1/2 teaspoon sugar
1 teaspoon salt
1 teaspoon cornstarch
1/2 teaspoon wine
1 teaspoon shoyu
2 slices ginger, minced

Marinate chicken for 30 minutes at room temperature. Spread chicken and mushrooms evenly in a heatproof dish. Steam for 30 minutes on a round cake rack in a large, covered pan filled with 2 inches water. Transfer to serving dish. Top with diced green onion.

■ OYSTER SAUCE CHICKEN

Vegetable oil for frying
5 pounds boneless, skinless
    chicken thighs

Marinade
2 teaspoons salt
2 tablespoons sherry
1-inch piece ginger, crushed
1 clove garlic, minced
2 tablespoons shoyu
2 tablespoons sugar
1 tablespoon oyster sauce

Batter
1 cup baking mix (Bisquick
    or other brand)
1 cup water
1 egg
1/3 cup cooking oil
1/3 cup cornstarch

Mix chicken with marinade and let sit overnight.

Dip chicken in batter and deep-fry until golden brown. Drain and serve.

■ HOISIN CHICKEN

At first glance the marinade looks overwhelmingly rich, but it is not.

2 pounds boned, skinned
    chicken thighs

Marinade
1/3 cup hoisin sauce
1/3 cup shoyu
2/3 cup brown sugar
1/4 cup sherry
1/2 teaspoon salt
5 to 6 cloves garlic, minced
1 tablespoon ginger,
    minced

Leave chicken overnight in marinade. Bake at 350 degrees for 30 to 40 minutes.

■ CHICKEN with BLACK BEANS

1 tablespoon vegetable oil
1/3 cup black bean sauce
5 cloves garlic, crushed
5 pounds skinless, boneless
    chicken thighs, halved
1 large round onion cut
    into eight pieces
2 green peppers cut into
    eight pieces
2 tablespoons cornstarch
1/3 cup water
1 1/2 teaspoons sugar
1 tablespoon oyster sauce

Heat oil and add black bean sauce and garlic; cook 2 minutes. Add chicken and sauté until almost done. Add chopped onions and peppers. Mix cornstarch and water with sugar and oyster sauce. Add to chicken and cook until thickened.

■ SWEET-SOUR BARBEQUE CHICKEN WINGS

This is also an easy pūpū that can be done ahead, frozen, and reheated when needed. This is a great sauce for both barbeque grilling and for kālua chicken or pork sandwiches.

5 pounds chicken wings

Sauce
1 14-ounce bottle ketchup
1 8-ounce can tomato sauce
1 cup cider vinegar
Dash Worcestershire sauce
1 teaspoon dry Colman's
    mustard
1 teaspoon ground ginger
1 cup brown sugar
1 cup white sugar

Lay chicken in large baking pan and cover with sauce. Bake uncovered at 350 degrees for 2 hours, turning once. Wings are ready when sauce has cooked down and wings are well glazed.

■ POT ROAST CHICKEN

This dish is quite tasty. Adding water to the remaining seasonings gives just the right touch to this wonderful dish. Our dear first neighbor, Teddi M., shared this recipe with me when I was first learning how to cook.

3 pounds chicken thighs
2 tablespoons vegetable oil
½ cup water
2 tablespoons shoyu
1 teaspoon sugar
1 slice ginger, minced
1 tablespoon wine
1 clove garlic, chopped
1 teaspoon salt
2 teaspoons cornstarch
   mixed with 1 tablespoon
   water

Rub chicken with seasonings and brown in hot pan with 2 tablespoons oil. Drain most of fat. Add ½ cup water to remaining seasonings and add to chicken. Bring to quick boil and then simmer covered on low flame for 20 to 30 minutes. Thicken sauce with 2 teaspoons cornstarch and 1 tablespoon water. Pour over chicken and serve.

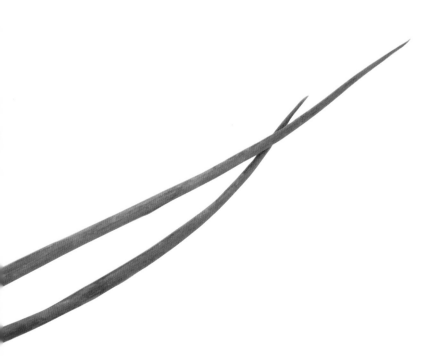

■ SKEWERED PEANUT BUTTER CHICKEN

2 tablespoons hoisin sauce

3 tablespoons peanut butter

1 teaspoon salt

1 teaspoon pepper

2 teaspoons peanut oil

3 tablespoons shoyu

2 pieces ginger, crushed

2 cloves garlic, crushed

2 pounds boneless, skinless
   chicken thighs, cut for
   skewering

Mix all ingredients with chicken and marinate overnight. Skewer and broil until done.

■ MISO CHICKEN WITH PEANUT BUTTER

5 pounds boneless, skinless
   chicken thighs

Marinade
½ cup miso
½ cup smooth
   peanut butter
½ cup soy sauce
1 tablespoon minced garlic
½ cup sugar
½ cup beef broth
2 tablespoons
   minced ginger

Marinate chicken overnight in refrigerator. Grill over charcoal or broil in oven until nicely browned and cooked through, about 10 minutes on each side.

■ KOREAN CHICKEN WINGS

2 pounds chicken wings

Marinade
4 tablespoons cornstarch
4 tablespoons mochiko
2 tablespoons flour
1 tablespoon salt
3 tablespoons sugar
2 eggs, beaten
2 tablespoons chopped
   green onion
2 teaspoons chopped garlic
Vegetable oil for frying

Mix all ingredients with wings and soak at least 8 hours, turning frequently. Deep-fry until golden brown.

■ KOREAN BARBEQUE CHICKEN

5 pounds boneless, skinless
   chicken thighs

Marinade
½ cup shoyu
½ cup water
3 tablespoons sesame oil
3 tablespoons sugar
2 tablespoons sesame seeds,
   toasted, mashed
4 tablespoons chopped
   green onion
2 cloves garlic, crushed
1 slice ginger
Freshly ground pepper
Dash Tabasco sauce

Blend all marinade ingredients. Marinate chicken in refrigerator at least 2 hours. Charcoal broil or broil in oven until nicely browned and cooked through, about 10 minutes on each side.

■ MISO CHICKEN IN BEER

2 pounds skinless, boneless
   thighs

Marinade
1 cup miso
1 cup shoyu
1 cup sugar
1 cup beer

Marinate chicken thighs in refrigerator overnight. Charcoal broil or broil in oven until nicely browned and cooked through, about 10 minutes on each side.

■ SHOYU CHICKEN

This is another recipe passed on to me by Lillian S. from Toshi H. of Maui.

5 pounds chicken thighs

Marinade
½ cup shoyu
½ cup vegetable oil
½ cup mirin (sweet rice
    wine)
1 cup sugar
2 teaspoons sesame oil

Mix sauce ingredients and pour over thighs laid in a single layer in a baking pan and bake at 350 degrees for 1 hour and 20 minutes, turning at least once during cooking time.

■ SHOYU CHICKEN WITH POTATOES

3 pounds boneless thighs
    cut into 2 to 3 pieces

Sauce
⅓ cup sugar
⅓ cup ketchup
⅓ cup shoyu
¼ cup sherry
½ teaspoon salt
1 clove garlic, chopped
2 inches ginger, sliced
¼ cup chopped green
    onion
2 medium potatoes

Cook sauce until it is boiling. Add chicken pieces and simmer for 1 hour. Add potatoes sliced ¼ inch thick. Cook another 30 minutes.

■ ROSEMARY-GARLIC ROASTED CHICKEN

1 whole broiler-fryer
2 teaspoons rock salt
4 cloves garlic, minced
2 tablespoons fresh
 rosemary, minced
 (or ½ teaspoon dried)
1 teaspoon freshly ground
 pepper
2 tablespoons olive oil
1 tablespoon sherry

Loosen chicken skin by placing fingers between skin and meat, beginning at tail end and gently working toward breast and drumsticks.

In small bowl, mix salt, garlic, rosemary, pepper, olive oil, and wine; rub mixture under skin and in chicken cavity. Tie legs together and place on roasting rack coated with cooking spray. Bake at 350 degrees until fork inserted in chicken goes in easily, about 1 hour and 45 minutes. If chicken is not done to your liking after cutting, microwave for 3 to 5 minutes.

■ JUANITA'S NO-NAME CHICKEN

4 pounds boneless, skinless
 chicken thighs
Flour
1 tablespoon vegetable oil
½ cup ketchup
½ cup water
2 cloves garlic, pressed
2 tablespoons
Worcestershire sauce
½ teaspoon ginger,
 chopped
1 tablespoon brown sugar

Coat chicken with flour and brown in hot oil. Drain half of oil. Combine remaining ingredients, pour over chicken, and simmer until chicken is tender and cooked through, about 45 minutes.

■ MINCED CHICKEN WITH LETTUCE CUP

This dish is similar to what you will find in Chinese restaurants. You can now make it at home and impress your family and friends.

1 pound lean ground chicken
¼ teaspoon black pepper
1 egg yolk
2 tablespoons vegetable oil
½ cup chopped bamboo shoots
½ cup chopped water chestnuts
1 tablespoon chopped shiitake mushrooms
1 tablespoon chopped green onion
1 tablespoon chopped ginger
1 tablespoon sake
1 teaspoon salt
½ teaspoon sugar
1 tablespoon soy sauce
1 teaspoon sesame oil
1 teaspoon cornstarch
2 tablespoons water
Vegetable oil for frying
2 ounces fried rice noodles
24 lettuce leaves

Mix ground chicken with black pepper and egg yolk. Stir-fry seasoned chicken in 2 tablespoons oil. Add bamboo shoots, water chestnuts, mushrooms, green onion, and ginger; cook until dry. Add sake, salt, sugar, soy sauce, sesame oil, cornstarch, and water; continue to stir-fry until almost dry. Remove from heat.

Fry rice noodles in hot oil in wok; turn noodles over to cook other side. Crumble onto serving plate and place seasoned, minced chicken on top.

Wash lettuce leaves and cut outer edges to form curved receptacles. Place in a serving dish next to chicken–rice noodle plate. Place fried rice noodles and chicken in center of lettuce leaf. Fold and roll lettuce leaf over filling and eat to your heart's content.

■ CHICKEN CASSEROLE

2 cups cubed cooked
    chicken
2 cups diced celery
2 cups cooked Calrose rice
$^3/_4$ cup mayonnaise
1 cup sliced fresh mushrooms
1 cup chicken broth
1 teaspoon chopped onion
1 teaspoon lemon juice
1 teaspoon salt
1 10 3/4-ounce can
    cream of chicken soup
1 4-ounce can sliced water
    chestnuts

Mix all ingredients and bake in
2-quart casserole at 350 degrees
for 35 minutes. Serves 8.

■ BEEF

BEEF with OYSTER SAUCE page 88

■ PERFECT ONE-HOUR ROAST

I was skeptical about this process but became a believer; I tried it and loved it.
You will too!

Beef roast of any type,
   any size
Salt and pepper

Take beef out of refrigerator in the morning. Begin preparing roast once it is at room temperature. Preheat oven to 375 degrees. Salt and pepper roast generously. Place roast on a rack in a shallow baking pan and cook for 1 hour. (If baking with potatoes, carrots, and other vegetables, add 30 minutes more to initial 1 hour cooking time.) TURN OVEN OFF. DO NOT OPEN OVEN DOOR. Allow roast to rest for 3 hours in oven to complete this initial phase of the cooking process. Twenty minutes before serving time, turn oven back on to 300 degrees to warm up roast.

■ JUANITA'S BURRITOS

This also makes wonderful won ton filling. One cup makes 20 won tons.

1 pound ground beef
1/2 cup water
1 bell pepper, chopped
1 green chili, seeded, chopped
2 stalks celery, chopped
2 cloves garlic, chopped
1/4 teaspoon pepper
3/4 teaspoon salt
1/2 teaspoon oregano
1/2 teaspoon coriander
1 15-ounce can chili with
   no beans
1 16-ounce can refried beans
24 flour tortillas

Brown meat in a pot, add water, and simmer with seasonings for 1 1/2 to 2 hours until tender. Drain excess liquid. Add chili and refried beans and mix well.

Place 2 heaping tablespoons of meat mixture on bottom third of each floured tortilla and fold over. Roll once, fold both sides in, and continue wrapping. Bake at 250 degrees for 40 minutes.

■ BAKED SPAGHETTI

This is an excellent dish for potluck and church functions. You can prepare it ahead and bake it at your destination for a hot dish that everyone will love. The creamed corn is an unusual ingredient and gives it a distinctive flavor. Serves 8 to 10.

1 clove garlic, finely
chopped
1 medium round onion,
chopped
1 teaspoon vegetable oil
1 pound ground beef or
turkey
8 ounces spaghetti, cooked
1 15¼-ounce can creamed
corn
1 8-ounce can tomato sauce
1 15¾-ounce can tomato
soup
¼ teaspoon white pepper
½ teaspoon salt

Fry garlic and onion in oil. Add ground beef or turkey and cook 10 minutes. Scoop out any oil or liquid from pan and add remaining ingredients, including spaghetti. Mix well. Bake in covered casserole or 9x13-inch pan at 375 degrees for 40 minutes.

■ EASY MEAT LOAF

This also makes 20 hamburger patties. Ground turkey is an excellent substitute for the ground beef, as is a soy-based beef alternative (see page 117).

2 pounds ground beef
2 eggs
1½ cups bread crumbs
¾ cup ketchup
¾ cup water
1 1-ounce package onion
soup mix

Mix everything thoroughly and bake in large loaf pan for 50 minutes.

■ EGGPLANT CASSEROLE

This recipe came from Lillian S., who got it from her sister-in-law, Toshi H., of Maui. It is similar to moussaka, only better.

1 1.5-ounce package
    spaghetti sauce mix
1 pound ground beef
1 large round eggplant
2 cups flour
1 teaspoon salt
1/4 teaspoon white pepper
1 egg, beaten
1/2 cup milk
2 cups bread crumbs
Vegetable oil for deep-fat
    frying
1 8-ounce package
    mozzarella cheese slices

Combine spaghetti sauce mix with beef, brown, and cook as directed. (Check sauce mix package ahead of time to see what other ingredients you will need.) While sauce is simmering, preheat oven to 350 degrees. Slice eggplant lengthwise into 1/2-inch-thick slices and soak in water for 10 minutes to remove acid. Dry slices and coat with mixture of flour, salt, and white pepper. Dip in slightly beaten egg-milk mixture and coat with bread crumbs. Fry in hot oil, drain.

Spread a thin layer of sauce in bottom of 9x12-inch baking pan or 2-quart casserole and add a layer of eggplant; repeat layering, ending with spaghetti sauce. Cover with mozzarella cheese and bake at 350 degrees for 15 minutes. Serves 8.

■ CHILI BEEF CASSEROLE

1 pound lean ground beef
   or turkey
1 small onion, diced
1 clove garlic, minced
2 tablespoons vegetable oil
1 15-ounce can tomato
   sauce
1 15 $\frac{1}{4}$-ounce can corn,
   drained
1 15-ounce can kidney
   beans, drained and rinsed
$\frac{1}{4}$ teaspoon red pepper
1 teaspoon black pepper
1 tablespoon basil
$\frac{1}{2}$ cup sliced black olives
$\frac{1}{2}$ cup sliced green olives
3 tablespoons chili powder
1 tablespoon chopped
   parsley
1 cup shredded cheddar
   cheese
Corn chips

Sauté beef, onion, and garlic in oil. Stir in remaining ingredients except cheese and corn chips until well blended. Pour into a 2-quart casserole, top with corn chips, sprinkle cheddar cheese on top, and bake at 350 degrees for 30 minutes.

GROUND BEEF or TURKEY with MACARONI SAUTÉ

This was my favorite dish to serve the 4-H girls who met at our house when Shari was in high school. One of them attempted to cook this at home, and her grandmother promptly told her that she had to cook the macaroni before adding it to the pan. The grandmother was very surprised at how well it turned out.

1 pound ground beef or turkey
¼ cup chopped round onion
1 clove garlic, minced
2 cups elbow macaroni, uncooked
3 cups water
1½ 8-ounce cans tomato sauce
2 teaspoons salt
¼ teaspoon black pepper
2 teaspoons Worcestershire sauce

Spray large pan with cooking spray. Brown beef or turkey, stirring to break meat into bite-size or smaller pieces. Add onion, garlic, and uncooked macaroni; stir for 1 minute.

Add remaining ingredients and bring to a boil. Cover and simmer over low heat about 30 minutes, stirring occasionally. Serves 8.

½ head iceberg lettuce,
  shredded
1 pound beef
⅓ bundle long rice
  (bean threads)
1 teaspoon peanut oil
1 clove garlic, crushed
3 slices ginger, cut fine

Marinade

2 tablespoons peanut oil,
  divided
1 teaspoon cornstarch
2 teaspoons sugar
2 teaspoons soy sauce
½ teaspoon wine
½ teaspoon ginger juice
  (juice from grated ginger)

Gravy

1 teaspoon wine
¾ cup beef broth
2 green onions, finely
  chopped
1 tablespoon oyster sauce
2 teaspoons cornstarch
¼ teaspoon ginger juice
½ teaspoon salt

Place shredded lettuce on serving plate.
Marinate sliced beef in marinade for 20
minutes. Cut long rice into 3-inch pieces.
Deep-fry one small handful at a time in
1 tablespoon hot oil. Fry both sides and
drain. Place on top of shredded lettuce.

Heat 1 tablespoon oil in frying pan and
fry seasoned beef with crushed garlic
and sliced ginger. When meat is nicely
browned, place on top of crispy long rice.
Mix gravy ingredients together in a small
saucepan and bring to a boil. Pour over
meat and serve.

■ OYSTER SAUCE FLANK STEAK

1 piece flank steak, scored
   on both sides into
   diamonds

Marinade
1 teaspoon salt
$\frac{1}{4}$ cup shoyu
2 tablespoons oyster sauce
1 tablespoon sherry
$\frac{1}{4}$ cup sugar

Place scored flank steak in zip lock bag in refrigerator at least 8 hours, turning several times to coat evenly. Broil 3 to 4 minutes on each side until desired doneness.

■ PORK

CHAR SIU PORK page 94

■ CHINESE-STYLE STRING BEANS with GROUND PORK

This is similar to the fried beans that you get at Chinese restaurants. Because reducing our oil intake is a good idea, I cook the beans in the microwave for about 5 minutes instead of frying. The dish tastes just as good and I know we are eating more healthfully.

1 pound string beans
Vegetable oil for frying
   beans
¼ cup ground pork
2 tablespoons small dried
   shrimp
¼ cup chopped Wei-Chuan
   or other Asian pickled
   cucumbers
1 tablespoon soy sauce
1 tablespoon sugar
2 tablespoons wine
Sauce from pickled
   cucumbers
1 tablespoon cornstarch
   in ¼ cup water

Cut off tips of beans and cut into 3-inch pieces. Fry in hot oil for about 5 minutes; remove and drain. Drain oil from pan. Reheat pan, stir-fry ground pork, add dried shrimp and pickled cucumbers, and stir-fry 30 seconds. Add string beans and remaining seasonings except cornstarch mixture. Stir-fry until most of sauce is cooked up. Add cornstarch mixture and cook until thickened.

■ PORK TOFU

This is a recipe from Hawaiian Electric Company. It has been an old standby since my early married days when I didn't know how to cook. I use this sauce for hekka (stir-fry) and oyako donburi (chicken and egg on rice).

1 pound pork, chopped
Vegetable oil for frying pork
1/2 cup soy sauce
1/4 cup water
1/4 cup sugar
1 medium onion, sliced
1 block firm tofu, drained, cubed
12 green onions, cut into 2-inch pieces

Brown pork in hot oil. Add soy sauce, water, sugar, and onion. Bring to a boil and simmer for 5 minutes. Add tofu and simmer gently for 3 minutes, spooning sauce over tofu. Just before serving, add chopped green onions.

■ BAKED SPARERIBS

5 pounds lean country pork ribs, sliced between bones
1 cup sugar
1 cup ketchup
3/4 cup shoyu
1/3 cup oyster sauce

Parboil spareribs. Remove, drain, and soak in remaining ingredients overnight. Bake ribs with sauce at 350 degrees for 1 hour, turning ribs once.

■ OLD-FASHIONED KAU YUKE with TARO

Trying this recipe brought back fond memories of potlucks at Pop and Mom Ah Moo's home in Kalaoa. It had been such a long time since I had this great "artery-clogging" dish. I was so happy to find the original recipe in an old family-style Chinese cookbook recently. I tried it and was taken back to the old days. Try it once and you will definitely want to make it again.

2 pounds belly pork
2 tablespoons vegetable oil
    for frying
Shoyu, as needed for
    coating pork
2 pounds Chinese taro

Marinade
1/2 teaspoon salt
1 tablespoon sherry
2 slices ginger
2 cloves garlic

Sauce
1/4 cup red bean curd
2 tablespoons brown sugar
1 tablespoon honey
1/2 teaspoon Chinese five
    spice
1 whole anise, mashed
1 tablespoon oyster sauce

Garnish
Green onions
Chinese parsley

Cut pork lengthwise into 3-inch-wide strips. Boil in enough water to cover. Simmer for 10 minutes. Rinse and soak in tap water to cool. Drain well. Coat with shoyu and fry until nicely browned. Soak in tap water again and drain. Slice pork into 1/4-inch slices.

Heat oil; stir-fry seasonings. Add pork and stir-fry 1 minute. Combine sauce ingredients and stir into pork until well coated. In a large bowl arrange pork slices, skin-side down, alternately with sliced, peeled raw taro.

Place bowl on a round cake rack in a large pot filled with 2 inches water. Cover and steam for 1 hour. Turn bowl over onto serving dish so gravy in bottom of bowl drips over pork. Garnish with finely cut green onions and Chinese parsley.

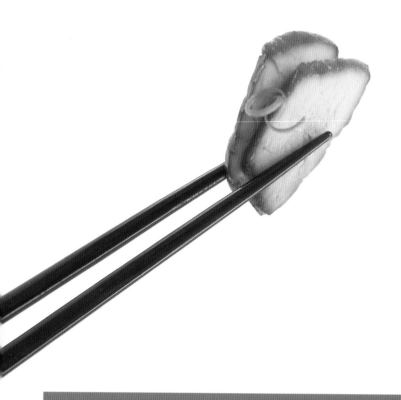

■ CHAR SIU PORK

This was the first dish I made with any success while single. Back then, in the '50s, pork butt was only 29 cents a pound.

1 pound pork, cut in 1-inch slices

Sauce
1 teaspoon salt
⅛ teaspoon white pepper
4 teaspoons sugar
¼ teaspoon allspice
1 teaspoon sherry
1 tablespoon soy sauce
⅓ cup char siu sauce

Marinate pork in refrigerator 4 hours or overnight. Roast 20 minutes on each side at 350 degrees in open pan or barbecue until well done.

■ PORK and STRAW MUSHROOMS STIR-FRY

1 pound pork, sliced

Marinade
1 tablespoon cornstarch
½ teaspoon salt
½ teaspoon sugar
1 ½ tablespoons shoyu
1 tablespoon sherry

2 tablespoons +
    2 tablespoons corn oil
2 medium carrots, sliced
    ⅛-inch thick
1 teaspoon minced ginger
1 15-ounce can young corn
1 8-ounce can straw
    mushrooms
¼ pound Chinese peas
¼ cup chicken broth

Soak sliced pork in cornstarch, salt, sugar, shoyu, and sherry mixture for 15 minutes. Fry pork in about 2 tablespoons oil; reserve marinade. When pork is cooked, remove from pan. Add 2 tablespoons oil and fry carrots and ginger for 2 minutes. Add drained young corn, mushrooms, and peas and cook for 1 minute. Return cooked pork to pan. Add chicken broth to reserved marinade and add to pan. Cook until sauce is thickened and clear. Serve hot.

■ PORK and BEANS and HAMBURGER CASSEROLE

Here is another of Yvonne Nagao's many fine recipes.

1 pound lean ground beef
   or turkey
1 medium onion, chopped
Salt and pepper to taste
1 can (1 pound 15 ounces)
   pork and beans
1 12-ounce Portuguese
   sausage, chopped, fried
   almost crisp, and drained
1 8-ounce can tomato sauce
2 tablespoons pancake
   syrup
2 tablespoons ketchup
1 teaspoon Worcestershire
   sauce

Cook beef or turkey until well done. Add onions and cook until translucent. Season with salt and paper to taste and remove remaining liquid. Add pork and beans, sausage, tomato sauce, syrup, ketchup, and Worcestershire sauce. Bake in oven at 350 degrees for 1 hour and 15 minutes, uncovered. Cover and bake another 15 minutes.

■ SPAM™ or TURKEY HAM and POTATO SCALLOPS

1 $10^3/_4$-ounce can cheddar
   cheese soup
$^1/_4$ cup evaporated milk +
   $^1/_4$ cup water
1 12-ounce can SPAM®
   luncheon meat or turkey
   ham
4 cups thinly sliced potatoes
$^1/_2$ cup thinly sliced onion

Preheat oven to 375 degrees. Blend soup and milk. Cut SPAM® luncheon meat or ham into julienne strips. In 2-quart casserole layer potatoes, onion, meat, and soup mixture twice. Cover and bake for 1 hour. Uncover and bake another 15 minutes longer or until potatoes are done.

■ MINI LAULAUS

Doris Sugihara shared her idea of using the whole seasoned pork butt as a laulau and steaming it. I first saw Margie Hirokawa serving it as mini laulaus at a church potluck.

2 pounds small luau leaves
(Hawaiian taro), about
6 inches square
4 large ti leaves
2 pounds Frank's Foods
Oven Ready Deli Roll■

Wash luau and ti leaves; remove stems and fibrous parts of veins. Cut pork into 1-inch cubes. Place 2 ti leaves side by side in center of 30-inch length of foil. Place remaining 2 ti leaves, crosswise, on top of first two. Place piece of pork in center of each luau leaf; wrap tightly. Place bundles close to each other on ti leaves. Fold ti leaves over bundles; seal foil tightly. Steam in a steamer basket over boiling water for 3 to 4 hours, adding more water as needed. To bake, place foil package in a baking pan with 3 cups of water; bake at 350 degrees for 3 hours, adding more water as needed. Makes 45 to 50 mini laulaus.

■ Available at most supermarkets in Hilo and on O'ahu. Hormel has a cured pork product that can be substituted. If unable to locate cured pork roll, soak 1-inch cubes of pork butt in brine made with $1/4$ cup salt, $1/4$ cup brown sugar, and 3 cups water. Soak overnight in refrigerator, drain, and use.

■ SEAFOOD

SPICY GINGER and GARLIC SEAFOOD PASTA page102

■ CURRIED MAHIMAHI

Not having tried this recipe for decades, I recently made it for a family gathering; everyone raved about it.

2 mahimahi steaks
Salt and pepper to taste

Stuffing
1½ cups cooked Calrose rice
1½ cups bread cubes
½ cup chopped celery
½ cup chopped onions
2 tablespoons snipped
    parsley
¾ teaspoon curry powder
2 tablespoons melted butter
1 teaspoon salt

Sauce
3 tablespoons melted butter
2 tablespoons snipped
    parsley
½ cup sherry

Season mahimahi steaks or fillets with salt and pepper. Place stuffing mixture between 2 pieces of fish in a casserole dish with a cover. Pour sauce over fish and bake at 350 degrees for 45 to 50 minutes.

■ HOT SEAFOOD SALAD

1 cup cooked shrimp
1 cup cooked crab
1 cup chopped celery
1/2 cup chopped
   green pepper
1/4 cup grated onion
1 cup mayonnaise
3 hard-boiled eggs, chopped
1 teaspoon Worcestershire
   sauce
1/2 teaspoon salt
1/4 teaspoon pepper
2 cups bread crumbs
8 tablespoons butter,
   melted
1 2-ounce package (1/3 cup)
   slivered almonds

Mix together all ingredients except bread crumbs, butter, and almonds. Pour into 2-quart casserole and top with buttered bread crumbs and slivered almonds. Bake at 350 degrees for 35 minutes.

■ ORIENTAL NITSUKE BUTTERFISH

1 pound butterfish or
   salmon fillet
2 tablespoons shoyu
2 tablespoons washed
   raw sugar
1 clove garlic, crushed
1 1/2 tablespoons mirin
   (sweet rice wine)
1 teaspoon grated ginger
1 1/2 tablespoons oyster
   sauce

Combine ingredients and marinate fish in refrigerator for 2 hours. Cook with sauce in frying pan over medium heat until done.

■ JUANITA'S SWEET-SOUR BUTTERFISH

Juanita Yamashita of California, a friend of many years, loved cooking and shared this and many other recipes with me.

4 butterfish steaks
Salt
Flour
Vegetable oil for frying

Sauce
1/3 cup sugar
1/2 cup shoyu
2 tablespoons chopped
   green onion
1 clove garlic, chopped

Salt and flour fish and fry in oil. Mix sauce ingredients and pour over fried fish. Cover and simmer on low for another 5 minutes.

■ SALMON or TUNA PATTIES

2 medium potatoes
1 7-ounce can tuna or
   salmon
2 tablespoons washed
   raw sugar
1/4 cup low-sodium shoyu
1/4 cup chopped round
   onion
1/4 cup chopped green
   onion

Wash potatoes. Poke holes in them with a fork and microwave for 5 minutes on one side. Turn over and microwave until they are soft to the touch, another 5 to 6 minutes. Remove from microwave and seal in foil. Let sit for 10 minutes. Peel under running water and mash. Add flaked tuna or salmon, washed raw sugar, shoyu, round onion, and green onion. Mix well and form into patties. Spray fry pan with cooking spray and fry patties in hot pan for 2 minutes. Remove pan from stove, spray each patty with additional cooking spray, and turn patties over. Cook another 2 minutes until nicely browned. Makes 12 patties.

■ SPICY GINGER AND GARLIC SEAFOOD PASTA

1 pound dry angel hair pasta
1 teaspoon grated ginger
1 tablespoon minced ginger
1 teaspoon chopped garlic
2 teaspoons vegetable oil
1 pound shrimp, cleaned,
    with tails removed
1 tray scallops (³/₄ pound)
½ pound firm fish, such as
    ono, 'ahi, or marlin,
    chopped into 1-inch squares

Sauce
1 12-ounce can chicken broth
1 cup water
¼ cup sherry
³/₄ cup rice vinegar
2 tablespoons oyster sauce
³/₄ cup sugar
½ cup ketchup
¼ cup Korean BBQ sauce
    (page 26)
2 tablespoons cornstarch
2 tablespoons water

Break pasta in half and add to boiling water. Stir to prevent clumping. Cover and turn off burner. Leave pot on burner and let sit for 10 minutes without taking off cover. Stir once after 10 minutes, drain, and keep pasta warm by covering with plastic wrap and placing pot cover over colander.

To prepare sauce, combine all ingredients except cornstarch and water in medium saucepan and bring to a boil.

In large saucepan sauté grated ginger, minced ginger, and garlic in oil. Add seafood. Cook until garlic and ginger are browned and seafood is half-cooked. Add sauce and bring to a boil. Taste and adjust flavors accordingly. Add cornstarch and water mixture to thicken. Toss sauce with pasta. Serves 8

■ EARL KEKUNA'S BAKED or BROILED SALMON ALASKA-STYLE

For many years, Earl lived in Alaska, where he picked up this recipe. It is a novel way of preparing salmon.

3 pounds salmon fillet
1/2 teaspoon white pepper
1 teaspoon garlic salt
2 cups brown sugar
8 tablespoons butter, melted
2 teaspoons liquid smoke
7 tablespoons lemon juice

Lay salmon fillet on a piece of foil large enough to wrap and bake fish in. Sprinkle lightly with white pepper and garlic salt and smother with brown sugar. Cover and refrigerate overnight. Mixture will turn watery, but that is okay.

The next day, mix melted butter, liquid smoke, and lemon juice and pour over fish. Wrap tightly in same foil and bake at 300 degrees for 50 minutes or broil until done. Baste with juices while baking.

■ SALMON BAKE

3/4 cup shoyu
1/2 cup sugar
1 tablespoon minced garlic
1/4 cup sesame oil
1/4 cup salad oil
4 salmon steaks

Mix shoyu, sugar, garlic, and both oils and marinate fish, meat-side down, for 4 hours in refrigerator. Bake at 350 degrees, skin-side down in sauce, until done, 30 to 40 minutes, or broil.

Serve over boiled cabbage or won bok (Chinese cabbage).

■ TERIYAKI SWEET-SOUR 'AHI BELLY

This is a delicious way to serve 'ahi belly, which is hard to come by these days. If you can find this delicacy, it's worth the price.

2 pounds 'ahi belly, cut into
    2-inch chunks
Flour
2 eggs, beaten

Marinade
1/3 cup shoyu
1/4 cup sugar
1 clove garlic, crushed
1/2 -inch piece ginger,
    crushed

Sauce
3/4 cup sugar
1/2 cup distilled vinegar
1/4 cup pineapple juice
2 tablespoons shoyu
3 tablespoons ketchup
1/2 teaspoon salt

Place chunks of 'ahi belly in marinade overnight in refrigerator. When ready to cook, dredge fish in flour, dip in egg, and fry until golden brown on all sides. Mix sauce ingredients, pour over fried 'ahi in saucepan, and bring to a boil. simmer gently for 10 minutes, tossing to mix to prevent fish from breaking up.

■ BAKED AKU or 'AHI

2 Hawaiian peppers
4 cloves garlic
2 tablespoons salt
4 pounds aku or 'ahi

Basting Sauce
1/2 cup shoyu
1/2 cup water
1 tablespoon sugar

Crush peppers and garlic and mix with salt. Rub fish, skin-side down, with crushed garlic mixture. Refrigerate for 2 to 3 hours.

Heat oven to 300 degrees. Place fish in baking pan and bake for 20 minutes. Turn fish over and bake another 20 minutes; pour basting sauce over meaty side of fish. Bake another 15 minutes, basting occasionally.

■ FUMI'S STEAMED MULLET with BLACK BEAN SAUCE

My late sister-in-law, Fumi, made this wonderful dish at family gatherings with mullet caught by my brother Mori.

½ 8-ounce jar black bean garlic sauce
2½ tablespoons vegetable oil
2 tablespoons sugar
2 teaspoons oyster sauce
2 teaspoons grated ginger
2 to 3 pounds mullet, cleaned
Chopped green onion for garnish

Mix all ingredients; rub mixture on stomach and exterior of mullet.

Lay fish on top of 2 large ti leaves laid lengthwise on foil large enough to wrap and seal fish. Place wrapped fish on cake rack that fits a large, covered pan and fill pan with 2 inches water. Cover and steam until meat flakes when punctured with a fork, 45 to 55 minutes. If fish is too large for pan, cut fish in half.

Garnish with chopped green onion before serving.

■ SIMPLY 'ONO STEAMED MULLET

This tastes like the mullet prepared by the famous Seaside Restaurant in Hilo, which raises its own fish.

Mullets
Round onions (1 thin slice per mullet)
Lemons (1 thin slice per mullet)
Pinch salt (per mullet)
1 tablespoon water (per mullet)
Ti leaves (1 per mullet)

Clean mullets; wipe dry inside and out. Lay on ti leaf over foil to be used to seal fish for steaming. Place one onion slice and one lemon slice on each fish, sprinkle with salt (use thumb and first finger), and add 1 tablespoon water. Wrap fish with ti leaf and seal in foil. Steam in large pan with about 2 inches water for 15 to 25 minutes, depending on size of mullet. Check water level while steaming and add more water as needed.

■ PAN-STEAMED MULLET

If fish is too large for your steaming pan, cut in half and steam.

1 mullet, cleaned
1 tablespoon washed raw sugar
1 tablespoon sherry wine
2 tablespoons low-sodium shoyu
4 shiitake mushrooms, soaked, slivered
6 green onions, chopped
2 bamboo shoots, slivered
½ medium onion, sliced

Clean mullet and pat dry. Lay ti leaf and then fish on top of a piece of foil large enough to seal fish entirely. Combine remaining ingredients and pour over fish. Fold ti leaf over fish and seal foil. Place in pan with 1 to 2 inches water and steam over medium heat for 20 minutes. Check water level and add more water, if needed.

■ SHIITAKE MUSHROOMS and ABALONE

2 teaspoons vegetable oil

6 large shiitake mushrooms,
   soaked in water and
   thinly sliced

1 8-ounce can abalone,
   thinly sliced

Sauce

$^3/_4$ cup chicken broth +
   abalone liquid

2 tablespoons oyster sauce

1 tablespoon dark soy sauce

2 teaspoons sugar

1 teaspoon wine or sherry

1$^1/_2$ teaspoons cornstarch

2 tablespoons cold water

Heat oil in saucepan over medium heat. Sauté mushrooms for 1 minute. Add sauce ingredients. Bring to a boil and thicken with cornstarch and water. Reduce heat to low and simmer 10 minutes. Add sliced abalone just before serving.

TOFU and OTHER SOY-BASED MEAT ALTERNATIVES
SURIMI TOFU TEMPURA page 114

■ STUFFED CABBAGE ROLLS

6 large Chinese cabbage
    leaves
12 ounces firm tofu
1 teaspoon salt
1 teaspoon soy sauce
1 teaspoon sugar
1/4 pound ground chicken
1 teaspoon sherry
1/2 cup spinach, chopped
1 1/2 cups chicken broth
2 tablespoons mirin
    (sweet rice wine)
1/8 teaspoon salt
1 tablespoon oyster sauce
Dash white pepper
2 tablespoons cornstarch,
    dissolved in 1/4 cup water

Wash cabbage leaves well. Shave outer parts of white stem if too thick. Microwave until tender and drain. Drain tofu and mash with potato masher. Add salt, soy sauce, and sugar; mix well. Mix ground chicken with wine; let stand 15 minutes. Mix chicken and tofu well; add chopped spinach.

Divide into 6 equal parts. Place each part at stem end of leaf; fold stem part over once, tuck in sides, and roll. Place cabbage rolls in saucepan, seam-side down. Add chicken broth, mirin, salt, oyster sauce, and pepper; simmer for 15 minutes. Add cornstarch mixture, stir, and cook until thickened.

■ TOFU TERIYAKI

12 ounces firm tofu, well
    drained
2 tablespoons soy sauce
2 tablespoons mirin (sweet
    rice wine)
1 tablespoon vegetable oil

Cut tofu into 8 1 1/2-inch-thick pieces; arrange in a shallow pan. Mix soy sauce and mirin and pour over tofu; marinate for 25 minutes. Heat oil in skillet; add tofu and fry on each side until golden brown. Remove from heat and serve on plate.

■ TOFU with FROZEN MIXED VEGETABLES

2 cups boiling water
Pinch salt
12 ounces firm tofu
1 pound frozen mixed
    vegetables
2 tablespoons vegetable oil
1 tablespoon + 1 teaspoon
    soy sauce
1 tablespoon + 1 teaspoon
    sugar
1/4 cup mirin (sweet rice
    wine)
1 egg, beaten, or
    1/4 cup egg substitute

Bring 2 cups water to boil; add pinch salt. Drop uncut tofu in boiling water and bring to boil again. Remove from saucepan. Drain water well; let stand for 30 to 40 minutes. Cook frozen mixed vegetables as directed on package and drain. Heat oil in skillet. Add vegetables and tofu; stir constantly until almost all liquid evaporates. Tofu will break up while cooking. Add soy sauce, sugar, and mirin; cook for 2 minutes. Add egg and stir until egg cooks.

■ OKARA PATTIES

3 cups fresh okara
    (tofu residue)
1 10 3/4-ounce can cream of
    mushroom soup
1 egg
1 6-ounce can tuna, drained
1/4 cup cornstarch
1 teaspoon salt
1 cup green onion, minced
Flour
1 egg, slightly beaten,
    for dipping
Panko (Japanese bread
    crumbs)

Mix first 7 ingredients well. Shape into small patties; dip in flour, egg, and panko and fry until browned on both sides. Makes 36 to 40 patties.

■ TAIWAN MUSHI

Lillian Sato shared this recipe with me many years ago. She claims not to be a good cook, but she is, as this recipe will attest.

1 pound ground pork or turkey
¼ cup chopped mushrooms
1 medium onion, chopped
¼ cup chopped bamboo
    shoots
1 block firm tofu, cut in
    1-inch slices
2 eggs, beaten (or ½ cup
    egg substitute)

Sauce
¼ cup sake or sherry
½ teaspoon salt
½ cup shoyu
½ cup sugar

Fry pork or turkey and add mushrooms, onion, and bamboo shoots. Add sauce and bring to boil. Place tofu slices in bottom of casserole dish; pour in pork or turkey mixture; top with egg or egg substitute. Bake at 350 degrees 35 to 45 minutes.

■ TOFU with MUSHROOMS in OYSTER SAUCE

1 20-ounce block firm tofu,
    drained
1 tablespoon sliced ginger
¼ cup chicken broth
1 tablespoon oyster sauce
1 4-ounce can whole
    mushrooms, drained
½ cup cooked green peas
1 teaspoon soy sauce
1 tablespoon sherry
Dash white pepper
1 tablespoon cornstarch
¼ cup water
1 green onion, chopped

Cut tofu into 1-inch cubes. Pour hot water over tofu and drain. Stir-fry ginger for 1 minute. Add chicken broth, oyster sauce, tofu, and mushrooms; cook until hot. Add peas, soy sauce, sherry, and pepper and continue cooking. Pour cornstarch mixed with water over tofu; stir and cook until thickened. Add chopped green onion before serving.

■ TOFU and SHRIMP with HOISIN SAUCE

Sauce

3 tablespoons hoisin sauce

2 tablespoons rice vinegar

2 tablespoons water

2 teaspoons sugar

$1/2$ teaspoon ground ginger

$1/2$ teaspoon cornstarch

$1/8$ teaspoon crushed
   red pepper

1 tablespoon + 1 tablespoon
   vegetable oil

14 ounces firm tofu, well
   drained, cut into
   $1 1/4$-inch cubes

1 clove garlic, minced

$1/2$ pound large (21 to 30
   per pound) shrimp,
   shelled and deveined

6 green onions, cut diagonally
   into 1-inch pieces

Combine sauce ingredients and set aside. Heat 1 tablespoon oil in large skillet over medium-high heat; add tofu cubes and stir-fry for 2 minutes or until lightly browned on all sides. Remove from skillet and set aside.

Add 1 tablespoon oil to skillet and stir-fry garlic and shrimp for 2 minutes over medium-high heat, stirring constantly. Stir in green onions and hoisin sauce mixture; cook, stirring until sauce is thickened and shrimp are opaque, about 3 minutes. Add tofu and combine well.

■ TOFU AND SEASONED CLAMS

$1 1/2$ tablespoons soy sauce

1 tablespoon sugar

1 tablespoon water

1 block firm tofu, cubed

1 6-ounce can seasoned clams

In saucepan, mix soy sauce, sugar, and water; bring to boil and add tofu and clams. Simmer 5 minutes and serve.

■ VEGETABLE TOFU SURIMI PATTIES

1 block firm tofu
1 container (1 pound) surimi
    (fishcake base)
1/2 teaspoon salt
Dash ground ginger
1 egg or 1/4 cup egg
    substitute
1 12-ounce package
    chop suey vegetables
Vegetable oil for frying

Cut tofu into four pieces; place one piece at a time in a cotton dishtowel and squeeze out as much water as possible. Mix with surimi, salt, ginger, egg or egg substitute, and coarsely chopped vegetables. Form into patties and fry in hot skillet with just enough oil to keep patties from sticking.

■ CHINESE FISHCAKE TOFU PATTIES

This is from my Honolulu 'ohana, which includes many good cooks.

1 tray (1 pound) Chinese
    fishcake ■
1/2-block firm tofu, drained,
    mashed
1 cup imitation crab,
    chopped
1/3 cup green onion,
    chopped
1 tablespoon oyster sauce
1 tablespoon shoyu
1 teaspoon sugar
1 teaspoon sesame oil
1 egg, beaten
Panko (Japanese bread crumbs)
Vegetable oil for frying

Mix all ingredients well, form into patties, dredge in panko, and fry in hot oil.

■ Prepared surimi (fishcake base) may be substituted if Chinese fishcake is not available.

■ SURIMI TOFU TEMPURA

This is a recipe my mother got from watching a Japanese cooking show. My children and grandchildren gobble it up as soon as it cools off. This tofu-surimi mixture will puff up nicely in the hot oil. It will deflate when cooled, but is very tasty. This is a good side dish or pupu.

12 ounces firm tofu,
    drained
2 cups surimi (fishcake base)
½ teaspoon salt
2 sheets nori
Vegetable oil for
    deep-frying

Squeeze water from tofu and mix well with surimi and salt. Cut 2 sheets nori into thirds, lengthwise, and then into 10 pieces, widthwise. Dip a teaspoon into hot frying oil, scoop a teaspoonful of this sticky mixture, and wrap a piece of nori around its center as you get it off the spoon and carefully drop it into the hot oil. The nori will stay in place as it cooks. Fry for 2 minutes and turn to cook other side for another 2 minutes until golden.

I have been experimenting with recipes using soybean products, to provide more healthful alternatives to meat. A number of products are available at local markets and from independent distributors. They need no refrigeration – just store them in your pantry. We like SuperSoy ground beef alternative, beef alternative strips, and chicken alternative strips. I have tried the following recipes on my family and friends, and they all agree that they can't taste the difference between the soy product and beef or chicken.

Caution: People on dialysis should consult their physicians before using soy alternative products.

■ MEATLESS MACARONI SAUTÉ

1 cup soy-based ground
   beef alternative
1 cup water
¼ cup chopped round
   onion
1 clove garlic, minced
Vegetable oil
2 cups elbow macaroni,
   uncooked
2 8-ounce cans tomato sauce
4 cups water
2 teaspoons salt
¼ teaspoon black pepper
2 teaspoons Worcestershire
   sauce
½ teaspoon washed
   raw sugar

Reconstitute ground beef alternative with water in microwave for 1 minute; set aside for 5 minutes. Brown onion and garlic in a little oil in a large pan with cover; add macaroni and stir for 1 minute. Add ground beef alternative and remaining ingredients and bring to boil. Cover and simmer over low heat for 20 minutes, stirring occasionally. Serves 8.

■ TOMATO WITH SOY STRIPS

1 cup soy-based beef
   alternative strips
1 cup water
1 cup chopped celery
1 cup chopped round onion
1 cup chopped green
   pepper
½ cup teriyaki baste
   and glaze
¼ cup ketchup
1 cup chopped tomatoes

Reconstitute strips with water in microwave for 1 minute; let stand for 5 minutes. Spray cooking spray generously in stir-fry pan and cook celery and round onion for 2 minutes. Add green pepper and cook 2 more minutes. Add teriyaki baste and glaze, ketchup, beef alternative, and tomatoes and cook another 2 minutes or until done.

■ MEATLESS CHILI

1⅓ cups soy-based ground
   beef alternative
1⅓ cups water
1 medium onion, chopped
1 15-ounce can kidney
   beans with liquid
1 8-ounce can tomato sauce
1½ cups water
1 1.5-ounce package chili
   seasoning
1 teaspoon oregano
1 teaspoon basil
2 tablespoons washed
   raw sugar
1 teaspoon Worcestershire
   sauce

Reconstitute ground beef alternative with water for 1 minute in microwave; let sit for 5 minutes. Fry onions in pan with cooking spray. Add remaining ingredients and bring to boil. Simmer for 15 minutes.

■ EASY NO-MEAT LOAF

This is the Easy Meat Loaf recipe with soy-based ground beef substitute. Use this recipe to make 10 hamburger patties. The kids will love this and won't know they aren't eating meat.

1⅓ cups soy-based ground
   beef alternative
1⅓ cups water
1 egg or ¼ cup egg
   substitute
1 cup bread crumbs
½ cup + 2 tablespoons
   ketchup
½ cup + 2 tablespoons water
1 package onion soup mix

Reconstitute ground beef alternative with water in microwave for 1 minute; let sit for 5 minutes. Mix with remaining ingredients and bake in large loaf pan at 350 degrees for 45 to 50 minutes.

■ MEATLESS SPAGHETTI SAUCE

1⅓ cups soy-based ground
  beef alternative
1⅓ cups water
1 medium onion, chopped
1 8-ounce can tomato sauce
2 cups water
1 1.5-ounce package
  spaghetti sauce mix
1 teaspoon oregano
1 teaspoon basil
2 tablespoons washed
  raw sugar
1 teaspoon Worcestershire
  sauce

Reconstitute ground beef alternative with water for 1 minute in microwave; let sit for 5 minutes. Fry onions in pan with cooking spray. Add remaining ingredients and bring to boil. Simmer 15 minutes.

■ MEATLESS BAKED SPAGHETTI

1 cup soy-based ground
  beef alternative
1 cup water
8 ounces spaghetti, cooked
1 clove garlic, chopped
1 small round onion,
  chopped
15 ounces creamed corn
1 8-ounce can tomato sauce
1 10¾-ounce can tomato
  soup
¼ teaspoon white pepper
½ teaspoon salt

Boil spaghetti; drain and set aside. Reconstitute ground beef alternative with water in microwave for 1 minute; let sit for 5 minutes. Brown garlic and onion with cooking spray in large pan for 2 to 3 minutes. Add remaining ingredients, mix well, and bake in covered casserole or 9x13-inch baking pan at 375 degrees for 40 minutes. Makes 8 servings.

■ MEATLESS TACOS

1 cup soy-based ground
   beef alternative
1 cup water
2 tablespoons onion flakes
1 1.5-ounce package taco
   seasoning
³/₄ cup water
12 taco shells

Reconstitute ground beef alternative with 1 cup water in microwave for 1 minute; let rest for 5 minutes. Mix ground beef alternative, onion flakes, taco seasoning, and 3/4 cup water and bring to boil. Reduce heat and simmer 5 minutes, stirring occasionally.

Heat taco shells in microwave 4 to 5 minutes. Fill with seasoned soy mixture and add **Southwestern-Style Guacamole** (recipe follows), low-fat yogurt, chopped tomatoes, shredded lettuce, and grated cheese to taste.

Southwestern-Style Guacamole

1 cup mashed avocado
2 tablespoons low-fat yogurt
3 tablespoons peeled, cored,
   seeded, and minced tomatoes
1 tablespoon minced parsley
1 teaspoon seeded, finely
   chopped jalapeno pepper

¹/₂ teaspoon ground coriander
1 tablespoon finely chopped
   red onion
2 teaspoons lime juice
1 clove garlic, finely chopped

Combine all ingredients; chill with seed from avocado until ready to serve.

■ SOY HEKKA

1 cup soy-based beef
  alternative strips
1 cup water
1 3.75-ounce package long
  rice (bean threads)
1 medium onion, sliced
1 small carrot, julienned
2 cups beans, diagonal slices
½ bunch watercress,
  cut into 2-inch pieces
½ cup sliced bamboo shoots
  (optional)
½ cup soaked, sliced shiitake
  mushrooms (optional)
½ cup low-sodium shoyu
½ cup washed raw sugar
2 cups water or chicken
  broth

Reconstitute strips with water in microwave for 1 minute; let sit for 5 minutes. Soak long rice in hot tap water for 15 minutes; drain and cut into 6-inch pieces; set aside. Cook onion, carrots, beans, watercress, and optional vegetables in pot with cooking spray for 1 minute. Add shoyu, washed raw sugar, and water or broth; bring to boil and cook another 3 minutes. Add strips and long rice and continue cooking until long rice has softened. If long rice absorbs most of sauce, add more broth or water and readjust seasoning.

■ SOY BROCCOLI

1 cup soy-based beef
   alternative strips
1 cup water
1 tablespoon cornstarch
2 tablespoons washed raw
   sugar
1 tablespoon sherry
3 tablespoons low-sodium
   shoyu
2 tablespoons washed
   raw sugar
2 tablespoons low-sodium
   shoyu
1 large head broccoli or
   2 medium florets,
   cleaned, chopped
2 tablespoons water
3 tablespoons oyster sauce
½ teaspoon ground ginger
   or 1 teaspoon grated
   ginger
1 tablespoon cornstarch

Reconstitute strips with water in microwave for 1 minute; let sit for 5 minutes. Marinate strips in cornstarch, 2 tablespoons sugar, 1 tablespoon sherry, and 3 tablespoons low-sodium shoyu for 15 minutes. Clean broccoli and chop into bite-size pieces. Let stand in salted water for 10 minutes. Drain and stir-fry in pan with cooking spray for 2 minutes. Add 2 tablespoons water and continue cooking 3 minutes. Add beef strips and season with remaining sugar, low-sodium shoyu, oyster sauce, and grated ginger and cook another 3 minutes. Thicken with cornstarch and water. Serve hot.

■ MEATLESS BEEF STEW

1⅓ cups soy-based beef
    alternative strips

1⅓ cups water

3 large carrots, cubed to
    match strip size

3 large potatoes, cubed to
    match strip size

1 large onion, cut in chunks

2 stalks celery and tops,
    chopped

2 8-ounce cans tomato sauce

2 cups water

1 10.5-ounce can beef broth
    (or 1 cup water)

1 14.5-ounce can chopped
    tomatoes

2 cloves garlic, crushed

3 1-inch slices ginger

1 tablespoon rock salt

2 tablespoons washed
    raw sugar

1 teaspoon oregano

1 teaspoon basil

1 bay leaf

2 teaspoons Worcestershire
    sauce

1 cup applesauce

Reconstitute strips in water in microwave for 1 minute; let sit 5 minutes. Microwave carrots and potatoes 3 to 4 minutes each; set aside. Chop onion and celery and brown with garlic and ginger in large pot with cooking spray. Add tomato sauce, water, beef broth or water, and chopped tomatoes; add seasonings and bring to boil. Add strips and partially cooked potatoes, carrots, and applesauce. (The applesauce helps cut the acidity of the tomatoes.) Continue cooking until vegetables are done.

■ This cooks so much faster than a beef stew. The amazing thing is that the strips do not disintegrate or turn mushy even after cooking for over an hour. You can adapt this recipe to make Portuguese Bean Soup by adding chunks of turkey ham, ½ cup uncooked macaroni, 2 cans kidney beans, drained, and another ½ to 1 cup water or beef broth. The macaroni will absorb much of the liquid. Adjust liquid accordingly.

■ SOY CURRY

1 cup soy-based chicken
  alternative strips or
  ½ cup soy-based beef
  alternative strips
Water to reconstitute strips:
  1 cup for chicken, ½ cup
  for beef
4 tablespoons margarine
3 cloves garlic, chopped
2-inch piece ginger,
  chopped
1 large onion, chopped
3 tablespoons curry powder
1 teaspoon brown sugar
3 tablespoons flour
1 12-ounce can Mendonca's
  frozen coconut milk
12 ounces skim milk or
  soy milk substitute
1 teaspoon salt
2 medium potatoes, cut
  into bite-size pieces
1 medium carrot, cut into
  bite-size pieces

Reconstitute strips. If using chicken strips, fry in 3 tablespoons hot oil for 3 minutes. Set aside. Microwave potatoes and carrots for 4 to 5 minutes until nearly cooked; set aside.

Melt margarine in large pot. Add garlic, ginger, and onion and cook until limp. Mix in curry powder, sugar, and flour. Add coconut milk and skim or soy milk substitute, stirring constantly. Add strips, potatoes, carrots, and salt and continue cooking another 5 minutes or until vegetables are done, stirring to prevent burning. Adjust seasoning, adding more salt and curry if desired.

Condiments: Chopped peanuts, crisp bacon, chopped eggs, candied ginger, grated coconut or mango chutney.

■ SOY STRIPS WITH TOFU

½ cup soy-based chicken
   alternative strips
¾ cup water
1 large round onion, sliced
½ cup water
¼ cup washed raw sugar
¼ cup low-sodium shoyu
1 20-ounce tub firm tofu,
   drained, cubed
2 green onions, chopped in
   1½-inch pieces

Reconstitute chicken strips with ¾ cup water for 1 minute; let sit for 5 minutes. Cut strips into halves or thirds. Cook onion for 2 minutes in wok pan sprayed with cooking spray. Add ½ cup water, washed raw sugar, and low-sodium shoyu and bring to boil. Add strips and tofu and continue cooking, spooning sauce over tofu for 2 to 3 minutes. If you prefer more sauce, double seasonings. Stir in green onions just before serving.

■ Chicken strips absorb more water than beef strips. Drain any remaining water.

■ SOY CHOW MEIN

1 4-ounce package cake
   noodles
⅓ cup water
1 cup soy-based chicken
   alternative strips
¾ cup water
2 tablespoons vegetable oil
1 cup slivered carrots
½ cup sliced round onion
½ cup string beans,
   cleaned, cut diagonally
   into pieces ¼-inch wide
   and 1½ to 2 inches long
¼ cup slivered cabbage
½ cup stir-fry sauce
¼ cup cooking mirin
   (sweet rice wine)

Cover cake noodles with plastic wrap and microwave with ⅓ cup water for 5 minutes. Drain any liquid; let sit. Reconstitute strips with ¾ cup water in microwave for 1 minute; let sit for 5 minutes. Combine stir-fry sauce and mirin. Slice strips into 3 pieces. Fry in 2 tablespoons hot oil for 2 minutes, add 2 teaspoons stir-fry sauce and mirin mixture and continue frying another minute. Add vegetables and cook another 3 minutes. Add remaining sauce and cake noodles. Mix well and cook another 1 to 2 minutes.

■ VEGGIE STIR-FRY with SOY STRIPS and BLACK BEANS

½ cup soy-based chicken
  alternative strips
¾ cup water
2 cloves garlic, chopped
2½ tablespoons black bean
  garlic sauce
2 tablespoons low-sodium
  shoyu
2 tablespoons sugar
½ cup water
2 broccoli heads, cut into
  bite-size pieces
2 cups string beans,
  cleaned, cut diagonally
  into pieces ¼-inch wide
  and 1½ to 2 inches long
2 stalks celery, cut diagonally
  into pieces ¼-inch wide
  and 1½ inches long
1 medium round onion,
  sliced
2 tablespoons cornstarch
¼ cup water

Reconstitute strips with ¾ cup water in microwave for 1 minute; let sit for 5 minutes. Stir-fry garlic in pan with cooking spray; add black bean garlic sauce, low-sodium shoyu, sugar, and ½ cup water and bring to boil. Add vegetables and sliced chicken strips and cook; thicken with cornstarch and water and serve hot. Add ½ cup more water if you desire more gravy.

DESSERTS

CREAM PUFFS with 'ONO FILLING page 130

■ GRILLED CHOCOLATE SANDWICHES

10 slices firm-textured
    white bread

Filling

1/2 cup heavy cream

1 cup bittersweet or
    semisweet chocolate pieces

2 to 3 tablespoons butter

1/4 cup sugar

Bring cream to simmer and stir in chocolate; continue to stir until mixture is shiny and smooth and chocolate is completely melted. Let cool until thickened.

Butter one side of each piece of bread. Spread about 3 tablespoons of chocolate onto unbuttered side of 5 bread slices, leaving a bit around edges uncoated. Top with remaining 5 slices, butter side up. Sprinkle buttered sides of bread with sugar. Leave crusts on.

Grill until golden brown on both sides. Be careful; sugar tends to burn if heat is too high. Wipe pan between cooking sandwiches. Cut them into triangles and serve warm. Makes 20 triangle sandwiches.

■ CHOCOLATE CHIP PEANUT BUTTER COOKIES

*This too is from Yvonne Nagao and is a favorite of Daryl's and his former dorm mates'
from Irvine. I am now sending them to him three to four times a year to share with his
colleagues at the Mission Viejo High School.*

1/2 cup shortening

8 tablespoons (1/2 cup)
    butter

1 cup chunky peanut butter

1 cup white sugar

1 cup brown sugar

2 eggs

2 cups flour

1 teaspoon baking soda

1 12-ounce package
    chocolate chips

Cream butter, shortening, and peanut butter well. Add sugars and cream until blended. Add eggs, one at a time, beating until smooth. Add dry ingredients and mix well. Stir in chocolate chips. Drop by heaping teaspoons onto ungreased cookie sheet and bake at 300 degrees until edges are slightly browned, 15 to 20 minutes. Makes 10 dozen.

■ CINNAMON SUGAR PLUMS

1 cup shortening
1 cup brown sugar, packed
1 cup white sugar
1/2 teaspoon salt
1/2 teaspoon vanilla
2 teaspoons cinnamon
3/4 teaspoon nutmeg
1/4 teaspoon allspice
2 eggs, unbeaten
1 tablespoon cold coffee
3/4 cup chopped raisins
1/2 cup chopped nuts
1 1/4 cups sifted flour
1 teaspoon baking soda
3 cups rolled oats

1/4 cup sugar
1/4 teaspoon cinnamon

Mix together first 10 ingredients; stir in raisins and nuts. Add flour and baking soda; pour in rolled oats and mix well. Shape into 1 1/4-inch balls. Mix together sugar and cinnamon. Roll each ball in sugar-cinnamon mixture. Place balls on parchment-lined cookie sheet and bake at 350 degrees for 12 to 15 minutes. Cool about 2 minutes before removing from baking sheets. Makes 6 1/2 dozen.

■ KENTUCKY SPICE COOKIES

3 1/2 cups sugar
1 cup shortening
1 1/2 teaspoons cinnamon
3/4 teaspoon cloves
3/4 teaspoon powdered ginger
3/4 teaspoon allspice
2 teaspoons salt
2 tablespoons baking soda
1 cup dark molasses
5 cups flour
1/2 cup water
Sugar
Strawberry or raspberry jelly

Preheat oven to 350 degrees. Cream together sugar, shortening, spices, salt, and baking soda. Add molasses and blend well. Gradually mix in flour. Add water to make dough of pie crust consistency.

For each cookie, roll 1 teaspoonful of dough into a ball. Roll ball in sugar and place on ungreased cookie sheet. Make small indentation in top of each ball and fill with small dot of jelly. Bake for 8 minutes. Remove from oven and immediately sprinkle with sugar. Cool before storing. Makes 9 dozen.

■ TOFFEE BARS

This is the simplest dessert to make and you won't believe how crispy and crunchy it is.

16 tablespoons (1 cup) butter
1 cup brown sugar
1 teaspoon vanilla
2 cups sifted flour
1 12-ounce package chocolate chips
1 cup chopped walnuts

Cream butter and sugar; add vanilla and flour and mix well. Stir in chocolate chips and walnuts. Press into ungreased jelly roll pan and bake at 350 degrees for 25 minutes or until browned. Cut into bars while still warm.

■ CUSTARDY BREAD PUDDING

This is the recipe by which my husband measures every bread pudding. It was given to me by Helen Hoke, a gracious woman who has since passed away. This pudding is very good with whipped cream topping or plain. It can be served warm or cold. You will find that some liquid will seep out when the leftover pudding sits in the refrigerator.

10 slices day-old bread
4 tablespoons ($^{1}/_{4}$ cup) butter
1 cup raisins
$^{1}/_{2}$ teaspoon salt
$^{3}/_{4}$ cup + $^{1}/_{4}$ cup sugar
6 eggs, beaten
6 cups milk, scalded
$^{1}/_{2}$ teaspoon cinnamon

Toast bread and spread with butter while bread is hot. Arrange toast in buttered 9x13-inch pan in 2 layers: 6 pieces (2 rows of 3) on bottom layer and 4 pieces on top layer. Sprinkle raisins on top and between layers of toast. Stir salt and $^{3}/_{4}$ cup sugar into eggs; add milk and stir to mix well. Pour over toast gently and let stand for 10 minutes, pressing down occasionally to help bread soak up most of milk.

Mix cinnamon with $^{1}/_{4}$ cup sugar and sprinkle over top. Place dish directly on oven rack and bake at 350 degrees until knife inserted in center comes out clean and top is an appetizing brown, 45 to 50 minutes. Center will be puffed and will sink when it cools.

■ CREAM PUFFS with 'ONO FILLING

1 cup water
8 tablespoons (½ cup)
   butter
⅛ teaspoon salt
1 cup sifted flour
4 eggs, beaten

Bring water to a boil in a medium pot over high heat. Add butter. When butter melts completely, add salt and flour. Stir constantly for about 90 revolutions. (Flour will come together and form a ball after about 60 revolutions. Continue stirring for another 30 revolutions.)

Take pot off stove; cool for 4 minutes. Add eggs and continue beating with hand mixer for another 4 minutes.

Drop rounded tablespoonfuls 2 to 3 inches apart on 2 cookie sheets lined with parchment paper and bake at 350 degrees for 1 hour. Turn oven off and leave puff pastry in oven for another 15 minutes to dry out membrane inside shell.

Fill puff pastry either by cutting off top ⅓, filling cavity, and replacing top, or by using a battery-operated cookie press to perforate pastry and inject filling. Makes 24 medium cream puffs.

'Ono Filling

1 package instant vanilla
   pudding
1 cup milk or ½ cup
   evaporated milk +
   ½ cup water)
8 ounces cream cheese
8 ounces whipped topping

Mix pudding with milk; set aside. Soften cream cheese directly from refrigerator by mixing with hand mixer; beat in pudding-milk mixture and fold in whipped topping. Prepare the day before to give flavors time to blend.

■ *The original recipe called for the eggs to be added one at a time. This made the batter creep up the beater. The recipe also called for baking the puffs for 15 minutes at 400 degrees and then at 350 degrees for another 15 minutes. Then it called for rotating the top and bottom pans and cooking for another 15 to 20 minutes. Rotating the pans always caused the puff pastries to fall.*

My son-in-law, Rick, shared this recipe with a fellow employee, who mixed in the 4 eggs at once and baked it for 1 hour at 350 degrees. These changes did the trick, and the result is this excellent, no-fail recipe.

■ WHOLE-WHEAT BREAD PUDDING

Knowing that I am always on the lookout for new recipes, Moira Tanaka, who is very health conscious, shared this recipe with me.

4 tablespoons (¼ cup) margarine

5 cups skim milk

¾ cup egg substitute

¾ cup white sugar

2 teaspoons vanilla

1 teaspoon cinnamon

1 cup raisins

1 1-pound loaf whole-wheat bread

Melt margarine in milk on stove. Combine with egg substitute in bowl; add sugar, vanilla, cinnamon, and raisins and mix. Pour into 9x13-inch baking pan and add bite-size pieces of bread.

Let sit for 10 minutes for bread to soak thoroughly. Bake at 325 degrees for approximately 45 minutes or until a knife inserted in center comes out clean. Chill until ready to eat.

■ KONA INN BANANA BREAD

This is my absolute favorite banana bread. I have come across many others over the years, but this is still the best, most moist banana bread ever. I use apple bananas.

2 cups sugar

16 tablespoons (1 cup) butter

6 ripe bananas (4 cups mashed)

4 eggs, well beaten

3 cups cake flour ■

1 teaspoon salt

2 teaspoons baking soda

Cream sugar and butter. Add mashed bananas and beaten eggs and mix. Sift dry ingredients three times and add to banana mixture. Blend until nicely mixed. Do not overmix. Bake at 350 degrees for 45 to 50 minutes until toothpick inserted in center comes out clean.

■ Do not buy cake flour just for this recipe. To subsitute regular flour, before sifting remove 2 tablespoons from each cup. This will equal 1 cup cake flour. (This is something I remembered from my ninth-grade home economics class.) Makes 3 medium loaves.

■ NO-KNEAD MALASADAS

This recipe was given to me by Dothrae Victorine many years ago and is my family's favorite. It will be yours too because it is so simple and so good. You can now make malasadas every Shrove Tuesday (Malasadas Day). These will not be rancid or hard the next day—if they last that long. They also freeze very well; microwave them and enjoy!

1 envelope yeast (¼ ounce)
½ cup warm water
1 tablespoon sugar
8 tablespoons (½ cup)
   butter
2 cups warm milk
¾ cup sugar
8 cups flour
1 teaspoon salt
8 eggs, slightly beaten
Vegetable oil for frying

Dissolve yeast in warm water with 1 tablespoon sugar. Let rise.

Melt butter in pan with warm milk. Measure sugar, flour, and salt into large bowl. Beat eggs in separate bowl; pour in milk-butter mixture and add yeast mixture. Mix well. Add liquid ingredients to dry ingredients and mix well. (Dough will be very soft.) Cover with plastic wrap.

Heat oven at warm setting for 2 minutes. Turn oven off and place plastic-covered bowl in oven until dough has doubled in size, about 45 minutes to 1 hour. Remove from oven and set aside while you heat your oil for frying.

Heat 3 inches of oil in skillet and fry dough by tablespoonfuls. Each time, dip tablespoon into hot oil first, before scooping dough, so dough will slip off easily into hot oil. Fry until golden brown, about 2 minutes on each side. Drain. Sprinkle with sugar and serve. Makes 5 ½ to 6 dozen.

■ CINNAMON BUNS

2 envelopes yeast
  (¼ ounce each)
1½ cups lukewarm milk
½ cup sugar
½ cup warm water
2 teaspoons salt
2 eggs
½ cup solid vegetable
  shortening
6 to 7 cups flour, sifted
¼ cup margarine, melted
1 cup sugar
1 tablespoon cinnamon
1 cup raisins
Vegetable oil

Add yeast, milk, and sugar to warm water in large mixing bowl, stirring to dissolve. Add salt, eggs, shortening, and half the flour. (For light, flaky buns, keep dough as soft as possible, almost sticky.) Mix with wooden spoon until smooth.

Pour remaining flour onto work surface and spoon dough on top of floured surface. Work flour into dough by scooping it into middle and kneading it in, turning dough by quarters and doing same until all flour has been kneaded in. Continue to knead it by pushing dough with heels of your hands away from you. When dough is elongated, fold ends in, give dough a quarter turn and start again, adding more flour on your working surface as needed to keep dough from sticking. Dough is ready for proofing (rising) when it no longer sticks to your hands and has a shiny finish.

Place dough in same mixing bowl coated with solid vegetable shortening to prevent dough from sticking. Cover with plastic wrap and place in oven that has been warmed for 2 minutes and turned off. Let it rise until it doubles in bulk, about 45 minutes to an hour.

Remove dough from oven and punch down to remove all yeast bubbles. Cover and let rise once more in oven for another 30 minutes. Punch down once again and roll out half of dough onto a flour-lined surface about ³/₈ inch thick and approximately 10 inches by 14 inches. Brush with melted butter; sprinkle generously with mixture of cinnamon and sugar, add raisins, and roll dough, starting from end closest to you, until you have an elongated roll. *(continued on next page)*

CINNAMON BUNS, continued

Cut into 1-inch-thick slices and place in ungreased pans, barely touching; let rise for 30 to 40 minutes in oven. Remove from oven. Heat oven to 375 degrees. Return pans to oven and bake for 12 to 15 minutes. Cool and ice with topping.

Topping 2 cups powdered sugar 4 tablespoons milk 1 teaspoon vanilla	Thoroughly combine all ingredients with electric hand mixer.

■ FUNNEL CAKES

This is a novel dessert that is especially good to serve at group gatherings like Cub Scout and swim team events. I first tasted it in Boston while on a family trip years ago when the children were young.

Vegetable oil for
   deep-frying
1½ cups flour
2 tablespoons sugar
1 teaspoon baking powder
½ teaspoon baking soda
¼ teaspoon salt
1 egg
1¼ cups milk

Heat 2 inches of oil in 10-inch skillet. Sift together dry ingredients. Beat egg and milk; combine dry ingredients with wet and mix into a smooth batter. Batter should be very soft.

Use a funnel with a $^5/_8$-inch opening. Hold finger over bottom end of funnel and fill halfway with batter. Swirling batter in circles from center out, drip batter into hot oil. Make cake about 6-inches wide. Fry about 2 minutes on each side until golden brown. Repeat until all batter is used. Sprinkle with sugar and serve.

■ PORTUGUESE SWEET BREAD

This is my adaptation of an old Hawaiian Electric Company recipe, using potato buds instead of boiled, mashed potatoes. You can use this recipe to make healthful sweet bread by substituting margarine for butter, 3 cups egg substitute for the dozen eggs, skim milk for whole milk, and 3 pounds unbleached flour + 2 pounds whole-wheat flour for 5 pounds + 2 cups white flour. An added bonus is that it tastes just great.

2 cups boiling water
2 cups potato buds
6 tablespoons sugar
1¼ cups tap water
4 envelopes yeast
    (¼ ounce each)
16 tablespoons (1 cup)
    butter
1 cup milk
12 eggs
3½ cups sugar
4 teaspoons salt
⅛ teaspoon ground ginger
5 pounds + 2 cups flour
Solid vegetable shortening

Add boiling water to potato buds and sugar in medium bowl. Add tap water and ground ginger and mix well until warm; add yeast, mix well, and set aside.

Melt butter cut into 6 to 8 pieces in small pot with milk on medium-low heat. Beat eggs; add sugar and salt slowly. Add melted butter and milk and mix well. Add yeast mixture and 2 cups flour. Continue adding flour, a cup at a time, using a hand-held electric mixer, until dough becomes too stiff to beat.

Place remaining flour on your work surface and pour dough on top. Gather handfuls of flour into dough center and knead. When dough becomes elongated, turn ends toward center and give dough a quarter turn. Continue working flour into dough a handful at a time until all flour has been mixed into dough. If needed, use more flour to prevent sticking. Dough is ready for proofing (rising) when it no longer sticks to your hands and has a shiny finish.

Coat same mixing bowl with solid vegetable shortening to prevent dough from sticking. Cover with plastic wrap and place in oven that has been warmed for 2 minutes and turned off. Let it rise until double in bulk, about 45 minutes to 1 hour; remove from oven and punch down to former level. Divide into 4 equal parts and smooth into round loaf by pulling dough from center top to outer edge, folding it under. Mound dough as high as you can and place in 8-inch greased, floured pie pans. Let rise in oven once again until dough touches edge of pan. Remove from oven carefully to prevent dough from falling. Gently coat with milk or egg white and bake in oven at 300 degrees for 30 to 35 minutes.

■ AH SAN'S CHOCOLATE SPONGE CAKE

In the days when I could not cook or bake well, this was the one and only cake that I made. It is moist, does not need any frosting, and tastes like the chocolate mochi that is so popular today.

8 tablespoons (¹/₂ cup) butter
2 cups flour
2 cups sugar
4 heaping tablespoons cocoa powder
2 teaspoons baking soda
1 teaspoon baking powder
2 eggs
2 cups milk
1 teaspoon vanilla
¹/₄ teaspoon salt

Melt butter for about 2 minutes in 9x13-inch baking pan in preheating oven. Sift dry ingredients. In separate bowl mix milk, eggs, vanilla, and melted butter; stir until blended. Add to dry ingredients and mix well. Pour into original baking pan and bake at 350 degrees for 45 minutes.

■ BEST CAKE BROWNIES

Double the recipe and bake in a 9x13-inch pan. This is a moist brownie with a cake-like texture.

8 tablespoons (¹/₂ cup) butter
2 1-ounce squares unsweetened chocolate
³/₄ cup sifted flour
¹/₂ teaspoon baking powder
¹/₂ teaspoon salt
2 eggs
1 cup white sugar
1 teaspoon vanilla
1 cup chopped walnuts

Melt butter and chocolate; set aside to cool. Sift together flour, baking powder, and salt. Beat eggs until light; stir in sugar and then blend in chocolate mixture. Stir in flour mixture, vanilla, and nuts.

Pour into greased 8x8x2-inch pan and bake at 350 degrees for 30 to 35 minutes. Cool before cutting. Makes 16 squares.

■ TOMATO CAKE

This cake is perfect with boiled frosting.

16 tablespoons (1 cup)
   butter
3 cups sugar
4 eggs, separated
1 teaspoon vanilla
1 cup tomato soup
4 cups flour
1 teaspoon cloves
1 teaspoon nutmeg
1 teaspoon cinnamon
1 tablespoon baking soda
1 cup milk

Cream butter and sugar until light and fluffy. Add egg yolks, vanilla, and tomato soup and beat well. Alternately add sifted dry ingredients and milk. Fold in stiffly beaten egg whites. Bake at 350 degrees in a 9x13-inch greased and floured cake pan for 45 to 50 minutes.

Boiled Frosting

1 cup sugar
½ cup cold water
1 egg white
½ teaspoon vanilla
½ teaspoon baking powder

Cook sugar and cold water in saucepan over low flame. Stir until sugar dissolves. Continue cooking slowly without stirring. While syrup is cooking, beat egg white until stiff but not too dry. When syrup leaves a long, fine, hairlike thread when dropped from a wooden spoon, it is done.

Pour syrup slowly over beaten egg white, beating constantly. Add vanilla and baking powder and beat until stiff enough to spread. Spread on cold cake.

■ PUMPKIN ROLL

3 eggs
1 cup sugar
2/3 cup canned pumpkin
1 teaspoon salt
1 teaspoon baking soda
1/2 teaspoon cinnamon
3/4 cup flour

Beat eggs, add remaining ingredients, and mix well. Grease 15x13-inch jelly roll pan and line with waxed paper, leaving about 2 inches extending at each end. Pour mixture into pan; smooth until even. Bake at 350 degrees for 15 minutes.

Sprinkle clean dish towel with powdered sugar. Turn pan onto dish towel. Holding extending edge, peel off waxed paper, holding it taut and carefully lifting it away from cake. Roll cake lengthwise in dish towel and let cool for 10 minutes. Unroll and spread with filling.

Filling
8 ounces cream cheese
2 tablespoons margarine
1 teaspoon vanilla
1 cup powdered sugar,
   sifted

Beat all ingredients together with hand mixer, spread over cake, and carefully reroll cake. Wrap in foil and freeze until about 1 hour before serving. (Freezing gives it body and makes it easier to slice.) This will keep months in the freezer, so I generally make a double recipe and save one for later use.

■ OKINAWA PUMPKIN DOUGHNUTS

This is the Halloween treat that children get when they come trick-or-treating at our house. Many look forward to it every year. This tastes like Okinawa andagi (doughnut) and is just as good the next day.

3 cups flour
1¼ cups sugar
1 tablespoon baking powder
Pinch of salt
3 eggs
¼ cup milk
¾ cup canned pumpkin
Vegetable oil for frying

Sift together flour and other dry ingredients. Beat eggs; add milk and pumpkin. Mix together wet and dry ingredients. Drop by tablespoonfuls into hot oil. Fry until golden brown.

■ MARVELOUS CARROT CAKE

Evelyn Crabbe was gracious enough to share this recipe with me many years ago. She was a tester for Betty Crocker and had many interesting recipes. It is a surprisingly moist cake. The only difficult thing about this recipe is grating the carrots.

2 cups flour
2 teaspoons baking powder
1 ½ teaspoons baking soda
2 teaspoons cinnamon
2 cups sugar
4 eggs
1¼ cup vegetable oil
1½ cup chopped walnuts
2 cups grated carrots
1 7-ounce can crushed pineapple, drained

Mix together dry ingredients. In a separate bowl beat eggs slightly; add oil, nuts, carrots, and pineapple. Mix well and add to dry ingredients. Bake at 350 degrees for 50 to 55 minutes in a greased and floured 9x13-inch pan.

■ BLACK BOTTOM CUPCAKES

The center will fall because of the cheese filling. It won't be as noticeable if you leave the cupcakes in the oven with the door ajar after baking. Take out cupcakes once oven has cooled. These taste good regardless of how they look. Just don't overbake them and burn the cheese topping.

Cream Cheese Mixture

8 ounces cream cheese

1/3 cup sugar

1 egg, unbeaten

1/8 teaspoon salt

6 ounces chocolate chips

Cupcake Batter

2 1/4 cups flour

1 1/2 cups sugar

1/2 heaping cup instant
   cocoa powder

1 1/2 teaspoons baking soda

3/4 teaspoon salt

1 1/2 cups water

1/3 cup + 3 tablespoons
   cooking oil

1 1/2 teaspoons vanilla

Beat cream cheese, sugar, egg, and salt with electric hand mixer in small bowl. Stir in chocolate chips and set aside.

Sift flour, sugar, cocoa, baking soda, and salt in large bowl. Measure water, oil, and vanilla in another bowl and mix until well blended. Stir wet ingredients into dry ingredients and mix well. Fill paper-lined muffin cups 2/3 full and top with heaping tablespoon of cheese mixture. Bake at 350 degrees for 20 to 22 minutes. Makes 24 cupcakes or 60 mini cupcakes (Bake mini cupcakes for 15 to 18 minutes.)

■ PIE CRUST

1⅓ cups shortening
4 cups flour
1 teaspoon salt
5 tablespoons water

Cut shortening into flour and salt with pastry cutter until fine. Add water and mix with fork to form a ball of dough. Work remaining flour into ball of dough with your hands.

Divide into 3 equal parts for 8-inch or 9-inch pie pans. Dampen your work surface with a sponge. Lay one sheet of waxed paper on work surface. Flatten ball of dough into a circle with your hands; place a sheet of waxed paper over this and roll dough outward from center and by quarters to form a 9-inch diameter circle, 10-inch if you're using 9-inch pans. (Place pie pan upside-down on rolled crust. Dough should be 1 inch bigger all around.)

Peel off top waxed paper, place pan directly over dough, and turn it over using bottom waxed paper. Center dough on pie pan and carefully remove waxed paper. Mold dough gently into pie pan, fold excess under, and crimp. Prick bottom and sides of dough with a fork to prevent shrinking and puffing. Bake at 450 degrees until lightly browned, 7 to 10 minutes. Makes 3 8-inch pie shells or 2 9-inch pie shells.

■ CREAM PIE FILLING

This is a rich and delicious filling recipe given to me by Doreen Gomes. I use apple bananas for my banana cream pie, a treat everyone loves. When cooling filling in the pan and when refrigerating, cover with plastic wrap to prevent it from drying out and forming a film.

2½ cups milk or 1¼ cups
    evaporated milk and
    1¼ cups water
¾ cup sugar
½ teaspoon salt
3 heaping tablespoons
    cornstarch
6 egg yolks
1 teaspoon water
1½ tablespoons butter
¾ teaspoon vanilla

Place milk, sugar, and salt in saucepan; let mixture come to near boil. Mix cornstarch, egg yolks, and water and add slowly to milk mixture, stirring constantly. Add butter and continue cooking on medium heat, stirring constantly until thickened. Cool. Fill baked pie shell and refrigerate. (Save egg whites for another use. I never mastered the art of baking meringue so I don't attempt it anymore.)

■ AVOCADO CHIFFON PIE

1 package unflavored
   gelatin
¼ cup cold water
5 eggs, separated ■
1 cup strained avocado
   pulp
½ cup + ½ cup sugar
¼ teaspoon nutmeg
¼ teaspoon cinnamon
Juice of ½ lime or lemon
1½ tablespoons butter
3 drops green food
   coloring

Soak and soften gelatin in water. In saucepan, beat egg yolks and add avocado, ½ cup sugar, spices, lemon or lime juice, and butter. Cook over medium heat, stirring constantly until butter has melted. (Do not overcook or avocado will become bitter.) Add food coloring and mix well. Add gelatin and stir until dissolved; cover and cool.

Beat egg whites until almost stiff and beat in remaining sugar, 1 tablespoon at a time. Fold into avocado mixture and pour into baked, cooled pie shell; refrigerate until firm. Cover with plastic wrap to keep pie from drying out. Whipped cream topping is good with this.

Makes 1 9-inch pie. Double recipe for 3 8-inch pies or 2 9-inch pies.

■ You may substitute 3 eggs, separated, and ½ cup egg substitute.

■ LEMON CHEESE PIE

Crust

1/2 teaspoon salt

1 cup sifted flour

1/3 cup solid vegetable shortening

1 egg, slightly beaten

1 teaspoon grated lemon peel

1 tablespoon lemon juice

Lemon Cheese Filling

1 cup + 1/4 cup sugar

1/4 cup cornstarch

1 cup water

1 teaspoon grated lemon peel

1/3 cup lemon juice

2 eggs, separated

4 ounces softened cream cheese

Add salt to sifted flour and sift again into a bowl. Cut in shortening until fine. Combine egg with lemon peel and juice; sprinkle over flour mixture. Mix with fork until dough holds together. Roll out to fit deep 9-inch pie pan. Flute edges, prick, and bake at 400 degrees for 12 to 15 minutes. Cool.

Mix 1 cup sugar with cornstarch. Stir in water, lemon peel, lemon juice, and beaten egg yolks; cook, stirring until thick. Remove from heat; blend in softened cream cheese. Cool. Beat egg whites to soft peaks; gradually beat in remaining 1/4 cup sugar. Fold into lemon mixture and pour into pie shell. Chill.

YAM MOCHI PATTY

This is one of several recipes Yae Miyasato shared with me years and years ago.
You can't stop with one.

1 can (1 pound 8 ounces)
  yams
2 10-ounce packages mochiko
1¼ cups sugar
1 cup water + canned
  yam syrup
Vegetable oil for frying

Drain yams and reserve syrup. Mash yams in a bowl. Add remaining ingredients. Form patties and fry in ¼ inch oil. Brown on both sides.

BLUEBERRY MOCHI

This recipe fell into my lap. I found it on my buffet counter several years ago when
contemplating what dessert to prepare for a coffee hour for David Matsuura. I don't
remember ever seeing it before. It has since become everyone's favorite.

16 tablespoons (1 cup)
  butter
2 cups sugar
1 large can evaporated milk
4 eggs, beaten
2 teaspoons baking powder
2 teaspoons vanilla
1 1-pound box mochiko
1 can (1 pound 15 ounces)
  blueberry pie filling

Melt butter and stir in sugar and milk; mix well. Add eggs and stir in baking powder, mochiko, and vanilla. Fold in pie filling.

Bake in greased, floured 9x13-inch pan for 1 hour at 350 degrees.

■ MAUI MOCHI

This, too, is from Yvonne Nagao, who was originally from Maui. Everyone loves this mochi; it stays soft for days.

2¼ cups water
1 cup light (clear) corn syrup
1 1-pound box mochiko
1 18-ounce can mashed
  sweetened tsubushian
  (red azuki beans); makes
  approximately 40 1-inch
  balls
Potato starch

Bring water to boiling, add corn syrup, and boil. Put mochiko into a bowl and pour syrup over. Mix well. Wrap dough in damp, clean muslin dishcloth and place in top of steamer pan. Steam over high heat for 18 minutes.

Transfer hot mochi into same bowl, pound dough with wooden pestle (or whatever you have that will do the job) about 100 times until dough becomes translucent. Place about ¼ of dough onto working surface covered with potato starch. Cover remaining dough (in bowl) with plastic wrap to keep it hot and moist. Shape into a log dough on work surface and tear off pieces to form 2-inch balls. Cover log with plastic wrap while working on mochi pieces. Flatten and stretch each piece of mochi into 3-inch circles by grabbing edges with both hands and pinching, turning, and stretching. Fill with ball of azuki beans and seal by pinching together center, then outer edges, and pulling edges toward center. Make certain ball is completely sealed. Place sealed mochi in palm of your left hand and rotate between thumb and third finger of your right hand for a high, round mochi. Coat bottom with potato starch; place on pan lined with potato starch and tap top of mochi gently to flatten slightly. When mochi is cool, but before it hardens, place it in zip lock bags.

■ This mochi freezes nicely and can be thawed and returned to its original state of softness. Freeze mochi pieces in a single layer on a cookie sheet. Place in zip lock bags and return to freezer. When ready to use, thaw completely in a single row on paper towels, 1 to 2 hours.

■ MICROWAVE MAUI MOCHI

Microwaves differ, so you may want to experiment with this recipe once or twice to see how long you need to cook dough. It will be worth finding out what works. Keep mochi warm while working with it; cold mochi is difficult to mold. This mochi is not as soft as the steamed version and will not stay soft as long.

1 cup + 2 tablespoons water
3/4 cup corn syrup
1 3/4 cups mochiko
1 18-ounce can mashed
  sweetened tsubushian
  (red azuki beans)

Combine water and corn syrup and mix into mochiko. Pour into microwave ring mold, cover with plastic wrap, and microwave for 7 minutes.

Carefully unmold from ring and cut into 16 pieces. Cover pieces with plastic wrap to prevent them from cooling off. Stretch each piece into a circle; place azuki bean ball on each circle and seal. Makes 16 to 20 mochi.

■ STEAMED MANJU

This is an example of Japanese country cooking using simple, basic ingredients. It is almost exactly like the yabure manju we loved growing up.

3 cups flour
1/2 teaspoon salt
2 teaspoons baking powder
1 cup sugar
1 cup water
1 1/2 18-ounce cans mashed
  sweetened tsubushian
  (red azuki beans)

Sift flour, salt, and baking powder. Combine sugar and water in a bowl and stir to dissolve sugar. Add dry ingredients and stir to make a smooth dough.

Turn dough out onto well-floured board and pat to 1/4-inch thickness with floured hands. Cut into 2x2-inch squares. Place 1 ball azuki bean paste on each square. Pinch edges together to seal azuki balls and place pinched-side down on wet muslin dishtowel in top of steamer pot and steam for 12 to 15 minutes. Remove and cool on wire rack to dry bottom of manju. Keep covered to prevent it from hardening and crusting over. Makes 4 dozen.

■ BAKED AZUKI BEANS

20 ounces azuki beans
3 ½ cups washed raw sugar
1 teaspoon salt

Soak beans in hot water and cover for 24 hours. As water is absorbed, add more water to keep beans completely immersed. Beans are ready to cook when they have doubled in size and can be pierced by your thumbnail. Scoop water and beans into 9x13-inch pan with enough water to barely cover beans.

Cover pan with foil and seal tightly. Bake at 450 degrees for 1 hour and 30 minutes. Beans are cooked when they begin splitting. Remove any liquid left at bottom of pan.

Mash beans with potato masher; add washed raw sugar and salt. Mix well until sugar is completely dissolved. Cover with foil once again and continue baking at 400 degrees for another hour. (Edges start cooking first, so stir beans after about 30 minutes.) At end of total cooking time, beans should be fairly firm, with no liquid floating on top. If mixture is still liquefied, continue cooking until liquid has been completely absorbed, another 15 to 20 minutes.

Remove from oven, keep covered with foil, and let cool before storing in gallon zip lock bag. Azuki will turn very dark and harden if foil is removed during cooling, a process that takes about 3 hours.

■ This keeps in the refrigerator for two weeks or in the freezer for up to a year. Make a double batch and keep it in the freezer.

COOKING and HOUSEHOLD TIPS

■ **Rice:** When making rice in a rice cooker, for fluffier rice stir washed rice 2 or 3 times, from top to bottom, and cook. After steaming for 15 to 20 minutes, stir the rice, folding it from top to bottom, and wipe steam off the cover. This process will keep it fresh until the next day.

■ **Perfect boiled eggs:** Place a paper towel in pot. (The paper towel keeps eggs from hitting against each other in the boiling water.) Lay eggs on top. Fill pot with water to cover eggs; cook over medium heat for approximately 14 minutes, letting water boil for the last minute. Take pot off burner and set aside for 15 minutes. Cool under running water and, while eggs are still warm, gently crack each egg, rotating it on a flat surface, starting with the rounded end. While peeling, let running water fall between the shell and the egg white. The shell will peel like a tangerine, and the yolk will be a bright yellow.

■ **Perfect pasta:** Bring water to a rolling boil in a large pot. Place pasta in the pot, stir to keep it from sticking to the bottom, replace the cover, and turn off the burner. Leave pasta on the burner for 20 minutes. Stir pasta at the end of this time to break up the clumped-up pasta; rinse under tap water and drain in colander. This procedure works with all kinds of pasta.

■ **Long rice (bean threads):** Soak raw long rice in hot tap water for 8 to 10 minutes to soften and to shorten the cooking process. Cut into 6- to 8-inch pieces and add to hekka, etc. It will still absorb a lot of liquid, so add more liquid as needed and continue cooking.

■ **Microwaving potatoes:** Wash and dry potatoes. Prick with fork in about 12 to 15 places to prevent skin from bursting. Cook 5 minutes on one side for 2 potatoes; turn over and cook another 5 to 6 minutes until soft to the touch. For each additional potato add another minute. Do not cook more than 4 at any one time. Seal in foil and set aside for 10 minutes. Peel and refrigerate to keep potato from crumbling when cut.

■ **Bacon Bits:** Portion bacon fresh from the market in quantities for normal use. Wrap in plastic; place in a zip lock bag and freeze. Thaw the portion you need and cook. Slice bacon into thin strips and fry crisp for more uniform bacon bits. This technique will yield more bacon bits than if bacon is fried and crumbled the conventional way.

■ **Tofu:** Always cover leftover fresh tofu with water before storing in the refrigerator. If you plan to keep it longer than 2 days, boil tofu for 5 minutes, pour off the boiling water, and cool the tofu. Cover tofu with fresh water and refrigerate in a covered container until ready to use.

■ **Mushrooms:** Do not wash mushrooms with water. Crumple a paper towel or napkin and lightly brush the mushrooms clean just before cooking. Store in brown paper bag to keep indefinitely. Plastic will make mushrooms sweat and spoil.

■ **Strawberries:** Wash strawberries just before eating or using. Store in brown paper bag until ready to use.

■ **Fluffy scrambled eggs:** Nonstick frying pan should be sizzling hot. Wipe hot pan with a few drops of vegetable oil and pour in just enough eggs to cover the bottom of the pan; stir constantly until eggs are almost dry. Remove to serving dish. (They will continue to cook in the serving dish.) Continue to cook remaining eggs in the same manner.

■ **Fresh green beans:** If you have more beans than you can use at one time, cook them in boiling water for 2 minutes. Take pot off the burner and set aside for 2 minutes; drain, cool, and freeze. This procedure produces the next best thing to fresh beans when you need them for cooking.

■ **Frying with cooking spray:** Spray cooking spray on your nonstick pan before frying. Remove pan from heat and spray the top of whatever you are frying with cooking spray and flip over to prevent the unsprayed side from sticking to the bottom of your pan. (Be careful not to spray directly on the hot pan.)

■ **Preserving vegetables in the refrigerator:** Green leaf vegetables such as spinach and lettuce, as well as cucumbers, green onions, garlic, and ginger, will keep for 2 weeks or more if wrapped in a paper towel and sealed in a plastic produce bag. The paper towel keeps the produce dry and prevents rotting. Wash the vegetables when you prepare to use them.

- **Ripening fruits:** Place green pears and melon in sealed brown paper bag for 2 or more days, until the stem end of the fruit gives to pressure. Nectarines are ready after a few days, when soft to the touch. When a ring of honey color appears around the core, apples are sweet and ready for consumption.

- **Frozen foods in plastic bags:** Cut 1 inch off the top of your frozen food plastic bag and use it to tie the bag containing any unused portion that is to be refrozen.

- **Getting the most rise out of your cakes:** For higher cakes, let cake dough sit for 10 to 15 minutes before baking to give your baking soda and powder a chance to rise.

- **Crisp cookies:** Let dough sit for 4 hours before baking. This keeps the dough from spreading and producing thin cookies. I learned this over many years of baking 4 batches of chocolate chip peanut butter cookies at a time to send to Daryl. I noticed the ones in the last batch were higher and crispier.

- **Bug-free staples:** Store flour, sugar, and pasta in refrigerator to keep them bug free. Bay leaves in a bag of flour also keep bugs away.

- **Splatterproofing:** Spoon ingredients into a pot of hot liquid with a serving spoon or similar utensil to prevent water from splashing and burning you.

- **Cleaning fish:** Immerse the fish in water in a baking dish; scale and gut the fish. The scales will be contained in the pan and will not fly all over the kitchen sink. This technique makes for very easy clean up.

- **Clipping coupons:** Fold the coupon in the newspaper in half and cut out three sides, starting at the fold. You won't have cut ends sticking out from your newspaper making it difficult to refold.

- **Minimizing your trash:** When disposing of articles like facial tissue boxes, take the box apart at the glued ends, fold it flat and dispose. You will have less bulk in your trash bin.

- **Disposing of cans:** Wash and drain cans; nest the smaller ones into the larger ones. Always place the lid at the bottom of the can.

RECIPE INDEX

NOTES

NOTES

NOTES

NOTES